THE
TUDOR
HOUSEWIFE

To my Mum, Clare Sim, with thanks.

THE
TUDOR
HOUSEWIFE

ALISON SIM

Cover illustrations: Detail from A Kitchen Interior *by Floris van Schooten (Phillips, The International Fine Art Auctioneers, UK/Bridgeman Art Library; Apostle Spoons (British Museum)*

First published in 1996
This edition published in 2010

The History Press
The Mill, Brimscombe Port
Stroud, Gloucestershire, GL5 2QG
www.thehistorypress.co.uk

British Library Cataloguing in Publication Data.
A catalogue record for this book is available from the British Library.

ISBN 978 0 7509 3774 0

Typesetting and origination by The History Press
Printed in Great Britain
Manufacturing managed by Jellyfish Print Solutions Ltd

CONTENTS

Acknowledgements   vii

Introduction   ix

1.   Marriage   1

2.   Childbirth   16

3.   The Education of Girls   31

4.   Housework   46

5.   Food and Drink   62

6.   The Housewife as Doctor   79

7.   Women and Business Life   99

8.   Religion   116

Conclusion   137

Notes   149

Index   163

ACKNOWLEDGEMENTS

I would like to thank the following people for their help, encouragement and provision of chocolate:

Margaret Peach, Jenni McCartney, Liz Clarke, Jane and Geoff Gardiner, Paulette and Christopher Catherwood, Jane and Robert Hugget, Jane Malcolm-Davies, Samantha Doty and Julie Anne Hudson.

INTRODUCTION

The picture we have today of the sixteenth century centres around the Tudor court. Many of us are familiar with the magnificent portraits of powerful courtiers in their court clothes which can be found in museums and famous stately homes like Hardwick Hall. The images of Henry VIII clothed in cloth of gold, or of Elizabeth I with jewels covering her gown are powerful ones, and hard to shake off. The courtiers were the multi-millionaires of their day, however, and their lives were as different from the lives of ordinary Tudors as the lives of the modern super-rich are to most of us today.

Clothes demonstrate the difference very effectively. The costumes worn by the courtiers for their portraits were to the Tudors what designer original clothes are to us, that is, garments which very few of us will ever try on, let alone own and wear on a regular basis. The materials that went into them cost several times what many people earned in a year. Queen Mary, for example, owned one gown which cost £36 in 1557[1] and this was not the finest she owned. This was a huge sum at the time. Just how huge will become obvious when you consider that in 1544 the merchant John Johnson paid £8 a year to rent Glapthorn Manor in Nottinghamshire, which included both farm land and the pleasant manor house where the Johnson family lived.[2]

Queen Mary's dress was made of velvet. The vast majority of the population wore wool. English wool could be of beautiful quality, and the wealthiest would wear sometimes the finest grades. The fine-quality worsted produced in Norfolk in the fifteenth century is even compared to silk by the Pastons in their letters.[3] However, ordinary people could only aspire to the rougher grades which were not only cheaper to buy, but lasted longer. Working clothes did follow fashion as much as possible, but the excesses of the wealthy were just not practical. Trains, frilled cuffs, large sleeves and other ornaments were impossible for most Tudors.

Just as the clothes of the wealthy and the poor were very different, so living conditions varied a great deal between classes. Houses were still quite basic for most people. Sixteenth-century cottages today usually come complete with indoor plumbing and central heating and are considered very desirable places to own. In their original condition no modern person would want to live there. Most houses were timber-framed, with the walls filled in with wattle and daub which played host to all sorts of insects. The houses were often thatched, although the use of slates was encouraged in towns to try to reduce the risk of fire. Most houses still had earth floors, which of course were very difficult to keep clean. Window glass was still a luxury so most houses just had shutters over the windows. There was also very little privacy: it was quite usual to share your bed with several other members of the household. In towns the houses often did not even have a toilet, but rather several households would share a communal one at the end of the street.

It was only for those higher up in society that living was becoming more comfortable. In wealthier circles there was an increasing concern for privacy and houses were built with a number of small rooms, rather than a small number of communal ones as was the case in the Middle Ages. Wooden panelling made the rooms warmer, but it probably would not be lovingly polished, as Tudor panelling usually is today, but painted in very bright colours. This was an expensive luxury and those who could afford it lived surrounded by colour that we might find rather gaudy today. The Wolsey Closet and the chapel ceiling at Hampton Court Palace are examples of the amount of decoration and colour favoured by the rich.

If you had money, you flaunted it. The Tudors would have been very at home in modern-day Hollywood, as they too believed in aiming to have all that was newest and most expensive surrounding them. The rich hung their walls with tapestries, again made in the bright colours they loved so much. Henry VIII paid £1,500 for one set of ten tapestries, and they were not even the finest set he owned.[4] This was at a time when a skilled worker like a shipwright earned about £12 a year, and a man with an income of £50 was a gentleman. Even in his garden a Tudor gentleman did not choose to commune with nature so much as to subdue it well and truly with topiaries, statues and elaborate designs of one kind or another bordered with little hedges. What better place to show off his wealth to his visitors?

The houses, though, only tell us so much about the Tudors. To understand the way they thought, some kind of overview of Tudor society is necessary. It is impossible to know for sure how many people lived in England at the time. Governments were not interested in statistics in the way that they are today and such information as survives is taken from church records (which are often incomplete) and surveys done with taxation or military service in mind (which of course did not include anyone not liable for either, such as young children). Estimates suggest that there were only just under three million people living in England at the beginning of the century, rising to just over three million at the end.[5] The population was very unevenly distributed, with about sixty thousand people living in the square mile of the city of London, let alone in the suburbs which were growing up around it even at that time.[6]

The main industry was still agriculture, and even people who had some other trade, such as weaving cloth, also had a smallholding which provided much of their food. Those at the very bottom, the landless labourers, were particularly badly off as not only did they receive very low wages, around £2 a year, but they also had no way of supplementing their income by growing their own food.

Despite the amount of food which was home grown everyone was by no means self-sufficient. Other things had to be bought in. Even items that were made at home were not necessarily made in sufficient quantity to avoid having to buy from outside as well. People did make a certain amount of their own cloth, both wool and linen, but few people would cover all their family's needs. Cloth manufacture was, after all, a large-scale industry, and there was a healthy market not only for the high-quality materials worn by the wealthy, but also for the humbler ones that most people wore, which would hardly have been the case if everyone had been self-sufficient. Other items were also bought in. Increasing amounts of pottery were appearing on Tudor tables, although wooden plates and bowls were still very much in use. Knives, which every Tudor would have carried, were also unlikely to be home made.

Higher up the social ladder there was a large demand not just for items produced outside the home, but also for imported goods. Silks and velvets (which were made with silk thread at the time), sugar, citrus fruits, wine, glassware and best-quality armour were all imported luxuries which every wealthy family wanted to own. The wealthy were certainly not self-sufficient and did not aspire to be.

Looking back on the sixteenth century it is also easy to imagine it as a time of security when families lived in the same villages for generations and even in towns people would know everyone in their street. In fact large numbers of people moved around the country looking for work. Names come and go from parish records with surprising frequency[7] and it was very common for children from as far away as Yorkshire to be sent to London for their apprenticeships.[8] Tudor London was such an unhealthy place to live in that it was only the constant stream of people arriving looking for work that caused it to grow so fast.[9,10] Even in the countryside people moved around. At Terling in Essex between 1580 and 1619, of all the men and women who married and produced at least one child, less than one-fifth of the men and only about a third of the women had been born in the parish.[11]

There were also people who lived by travelling, such as carters transporting goods, especially wool, and those who drove cattle long distances to market. Even some skilled workers, such as shipwrights, lived by moving around from job to job, depending where the work happened to be at the time. Society was far more mobile than you may imagine.

Death was also constantly in the minds of the people of the time, so much so that there was a fashion for paintings, jewellery and a whole host of other items decorated with skulls as a reminder that anyone could be struck down at any time. The infant mortality rates in particular are horrifying.[12] In modern-day Britain we expect to raise all the children we have to adulthood, but this is a luxury unknown to previous ages. It is impossible to give exact statistics as accurate records were not always kept, and, even if they were, have not always survived complete. There is a high probability too that many children who died in the first few weeks of life went totally unrecorded. From existing records it seems that about a fifth of the children born in Elizabethan England did not reach their tenth birthday.[13]

Life was not certain at any age. Plague was never far away, or small pox, which often left its victims badly disfigured even if they survived. One disease, the 'sweat', which visited England several times in the sixteenth century seemed to be particularly fatal to the young adults, who should have been best placed to resist disease. The two sons of Catherine Willoughby, Duchess of Suffolk,[14] died from it when they were in their teens. Otwell Johnson, a young man who was a merchant of the staple, whose letters form part of a collection which reveal a great deal about Tudor life was also a victim.[15] The disease was particularly frightening as it struck and killed within twenty-four hours. Life was anything but secure.

The way society was organized was very different from today. There was no professional police force, and hardly any standing army apart from the king's personal bodyguard, which only consisted of about two hundred men at the most. Order was maintained through strict observance of the social hierarchy. The Tudors saw the world as a vast hierarchy where everyone, and everything, had its place.

Today we are brought up to question everything, to think for ourselves and to consider ourselves as equal to anyone. Tudor children were brought up above all things to show respect, to speak when they were spoken to and accept what they were told by their elders and betters. A Tudor child would refer to its parents as 'Sir' and 'Madam' and would stand up when they came into a room. They would treat anyone in authority, such as the master and mistress they worked for as apprentices, in the same way. The result was that they grew up with a view of the world that was very different to our modern one.

This idea of authority even existed in the academic world, where those who challenged views laid down by ancient authorities were frowned on. Medical thought was, for example, still dominated by the works of Galen and Avicenna who had lived hundreds of years before.[16] Those who challenged their views sometimes even found themselves forced to recant publicly. By the end of the century things did begin to change. The old views were being challenged too loudly and too often for them to continue to be accepted without question. It was no longer enough just to read and accept ancient knowledge. This spirit of enquiry laid the foundations for the scientific developments of the seventeenth century, but it had been a long hard struggle to awaken it.

You would be reminded of your place in the hierarchy at every opportunity. For one thing, you would be seated at meal times in a certain place according to your position. The etiquette books of the time go into great detail as to precedence in these matters. If you were responsible for the seating arrangements you needed to get it right or you might seriously offend someone. John Russell's *Book of Nurture*, a book written around 1460 for the instruction of children, goes into great detail as to seating arrangements, giving instructions for placing everyone from the Pope right down to a lady of low degree who has married above herself. Of course, very few people were going to cope with such a wide range of guests, and nobody in England entertained the Pope, but the idea was that children taught from Russell's book would learn how the social hierarchy worked.[17]

It was important to know who was above you and who was beneath you, and to behave with great respect towards great men. The aristocracy in particular had enormous power and their favour could make your career, or their dislike ruin it. It was for this reason that education centred on how to make yourself pleasing to your betters, whether by working hard or, at the top of society, by being able to take part in witty conversations and elegant pastimes such as formal debates. The idea of Renaissance man, the all-rounder who could hold his own in intellectual circles, take part in sport, show skill on the battlefield and still be able to dance, sing and play musical instruments, was not an ideal dreamt up by scholars. Such all-rounders would have been best-placed to win the attention and regard of those who mattered. Doubtless few people lived up to the ideal, but aiming at it was the way towards success.

As the Tudors saw that prosperity lay in serving those above you there was no disgrace in being a servant. Wealthy people often had very well-bred personal servants who might even be their relatives. Attending a great gentleman or lady was considered a very good way of learning how to move in the highest society and was often part of your education. This is why the Lisle daughters were sent away to live with a French gentlewoman.[18] Even lower down the scale service could be a good preparation for marriage[19] and a secure way of earning a living.

Even servants who were not gently bred were not looked down on. Although they would be expected to show respect to their master and mistress, they would not be considered second-class as they would have been in the eighteenth or the nineteenth century. You did not keep your servants hidden away in a separate part of your house. Your personal servants, whether relatives or not, had to be within calling distance at all times, so that you could summon them whenever required. They even slept in your room at night. Other servants could also be held in high regard. Otwell Johnson even held one of his apprentices, Henry Johnson (no relation of Otwell's), in his arms as he lay dying, even though it was suspected that he was suffering from plague.[20] Even Pepys, writing in the late seventeenth century, considered his servants as part of his family.[21]

All this sounds as though society was reassuringly stable in the sixteenth century but the theory of how society was organized didn't work out in practice quite how it was supposed to. For one thing, at any time in any society, there are always families who are on their way up in the world and others who are on the way down. Society was also becoming a lot more fluid. In the Middle Ages, for example in the thirteenth century, it was very difficult for anyone not born to wealth to achieve it for themselves. The Church did provide an outlet for an able young man to rise to the top, but that was really the only way for those who were talented but not well connected. By the sixteenth century it was possible to rise in the secular world, by trade or by a profession such as the law, so that new families, as well as individuals, came to prominence. The 'new men' of the Tudor age, such as Thomas Cromwell, even got into the highest circles surrounding the king.

Politics had also changed since the Middle Ages. Even as late as the fifteenth century kings had had to deal with enormously powerful barons. The exploits of Warwick the Kingmaker, who was literally able to influence the fate of kings, demonstrates this very well. Kingship involved a careful balancing act between demonstrating your own authority and not upsetting the barons too much.

By the sixteenth century this had all changed. Power was centralized in the hands of the monarch to such an extent that even at times of crisis, such as the accession of the young king Edward VI, such plotting and jostling for power as occurred was all centred around the court, rather than in the private castles of particular barons as had been the case in earlier times.[22]

The Tudor kings had power firmly centred in their hands. Government departments took over the day-to-day running of affairs, as there was too much business for the monarch to cope with alone. This meant that more educated men were needed to staff these departments, which in turn not only gave new opportunities to such men, but also stimulated more people to become educated.

The increasing bureaucracy meant more business for the lawyers, so that many Tudor fortunes were made that way. There was no land registry at the time, and most people who owned a significant amount of land found themselves involved in lawsuits of one kind or another with people who also felt they had a claim to their land. Legal training increasingly became part of a normal education for anyone who was heir to land. Education was becoming more and more of a necessity for the better off citizens. The middle classes were also becoming richer, better educated and more confident. Trade was expanding; the London merchants in particular were thriving and their children might well be educated for a profession such as the law. In this new atmosphere of self-confident enquiry it was inevitable that the religious views of the time should change.

In the Middle Ages most people were expected to take the religious opinions of their priest. By the end of the fifteenth century people throughout Europe were wanting to study the Bible for themselves, to form their own opinions. There were also cries against the corruption of the established Church, and against many of the accepted practices of the day, most famously from Martin Luther.[23] By the end of the century Catholics and Protestants alike were being encouraged to study devotional works for themselves. Richard Smith, biographer of Lady Magdalene Montague, a recusant of Elizabeth's reign, takes great pains to stress Lady Montague's hours of private study as well as her devotion to the Mass.[24]

The new interest in education was both symptom and cause of the printing press. This had come to England at the end of the fifteenth century and by the mid-sixteenth century a wide range of books was being published. Books were still fairly expensive, beyond the reach of ordinary people, but were nevertheless very much cheaper than the hand-written books of the Middle Ages. Reading was becoming a habit for both men and women of the middle class.

Family relationships were slowly beginning to change. It is very easy to misunderstand how the Tudors felt about their children. The fact that relations between parents and children were considerably more formal than today does not mean that there was not affection between them. Neither is it true that parents did not become fond of their children in case they died; there are many examples of Tudor men and women taking great pleasure in their children and being grief-stricken when they died. It was rather that they cultivated the Christian virtue of resignation, that is, of accepting God's will, however hard. This is a long way from not caring in the first place.[25]

Tudor children were expected to show a great deal of respect but there was an increasing trend to respect their feelings in the major decisions affecting them. This is particularly true in the area of marriage. Even amongst the aristocracy child marriages were dying out. Marriage remained very much a business matter to be arranged by the child's parents, but books of the time emphasize increasingly that a successful marriage had to be based on the willing consent, if not necessarily mutual affection, of the parties involved.

Despite the social change taking place, the daily round must have remained much the same for most ordinary people throughout the century. Hours of work were long, at least in the summer. An act of 1563 fixed the hours of summer work (mid-March to mid-September) from five in the morning to either seven or eight in the evening, with not more than two and a half hours for breaks.[26] In winter the hours were from dawn to sunset, as it was simply not practical to work by artificial light. The best-quality light was that from wax candles which were far too expensive for most people to use on a regular basis, if at all. Even lower-quality lights, rushlights made from tallow, had to be used with care.

For all the building of fine houses and the flowering of the arts that the Tudor period witnessed, it was a hard time for those at the bottom of society. The problem of what exactly to do about the increasing number of people who wandered about in search of work was one which troubled the Elizabethans in particular. The parishes were supposed to organize poor relief for those who were having difficulty so they were very unwilling to have any vagrants in the area unless they were gainfully employed. The result was that poor people were hustled out of the parish as often as they were helped.

Life was not easy for either men or women, but the women were often in a particularly difficult situation. A single woman was more or less a piece of her father's property; a married woman belonged to her husband in the same way, her possessions also automatically belonging to her husband. Widows were the only independent Tudor women. A woman was also at a disadvantage as it was much harder for her to earn an independent living than it was for a man. By no means all women married, but a woman who was single had far fewer options regarding apprenticeship and employment than a man did.[27] There were also fewer educational opportunities, so that women could not attend the universities or Inns of Court and therefore could not enter a profession. This gives the impression that the women of the time, barred from most education and many jobs, were ignorant and incapable. It is far from the truth. Several noble women of the time, such as Thomas More's daughters and the Cooke sisters were very well educated by tutors at home. Even women who were not academically educated were given sound practical tuition in the skills they would need to run their houses and, for the wealthy, their estates. Accounts, medical skills, cookery as well as the practical skills needed to help run a business were all taught to girls at the time.

The idea that wealthy ladies should be brought up to do nothing did not come into fashion until the eighteenth century. In the sixteenth century the feeling was that the devil found work for idle hands to do, whatever class the owner of the hands came from. Educational books for ladies are full of the need to banish idleness. The title page of the popular needlework pattern book *The Needle's Excellency*, reproduced in Chapter Three, is an example of the encouragement to useful work. Few women must have needed to be told to work. They had so much to do that they must have had little time to do anything else. Even wealthy women were very much practical, working housewives. They may have had servants, but these were people whom they worked alongside, rather than just gave orders to as the grand ladies of later centuries did.

The incredible range of practical skills demonstrated by the women of the time tends to go unacknowledged even today. The problem is that the sixteenth century was a man's world, and women left few records of what they did and thought. Even the household manuals of the time were written by men, such as Gervase Markham and Thomas Tusser.[28] Men were not taught 'housewifery' and so it was not publicly esteemed in the way that, for example, knowledge of the law was. The women's skills may or may not have been appreciated, but they were still expected to be able to cope with a wide range of problems. Their knowledge is even more impressive when it becomes obvious how much skill was involved in jobs which are incredibly simple today. The weekly wash could not only take two or three days to complete, but a woman would need to know how to treat various different stains, and possibly even have to make her own soap. She would not only deal with family medical problems, but would also have to make her own medicines. If she was wealthy, her husband could be away on business more often than he was home, leaving her to cope with the business affairs of the estates as well as the running of the household.

This book is only an overview of the lives of Tudor women. The subjects covered in each chapter could easily each be the subject of an entire book if not of a whole lifetime's study. The aim is to give a feeling of what life was like at the time for ordinary women, as well as the rich and famous women with whom many of us are already familiar. Perhaps it will also give a new appreciation of the incredible range of skills expected of women at the time.

ONE

MARRIAGE

The popular view of Tudor marriage is that people married very young indeed, and that the young couple had no say whatsoever in whom they married. In fact the age at which you could expect to marry, the amount of choice you had and even whether you could expect to marry at all varied enormously depending on your social background.

It is of course difficult to be sure of statistics at this time, but studies suggest that in Elizabethan and Stuart England the average age for women at their first marriage was twenty-six, and for men somewhere between twenty-seven and twenty-nine.[1] As many as one in six people were still unmarried in their forties, meaning that they probably never married. Poorer people had to save up before they could marry, so that they could afford somewhere to live and the basics they needed to set up home with. In hard times, like those at the end of the sixteenth century when there was a run of bad harvests, this could be impossible. For this reason there was often a boom in marriages in prosperous years, such as the years 1598–1605, but a significant drop in bad ones, such as 1594–97.[2]

Those who married youngest were from the wealthiest section of the population, in particular from the families with political ambitions. Royalty could find themselves betrothed, if not actually married, quite literally in their cradles. Henry VIII's eldest daughter, Princess Mary, was betrothed to the French Dauphin at the age of two, although the marriage never took place. There were also very few major land-owning families, so the number of suitable partners for children was fairly limited. Parents therefore tended to grab a good match, particularly for their son and heir, when it came along, even if the couple involved were very young.

The existence of wardship was another problem for major landowners. If one of them died leaving an heir who was under age, the wardship of the child was a piece of property. The owner of the wardship ran the estates until the heir came of age, and also chose the ward's marriage partner. Naturally parents feared that their heir might be forced to marry someone they would not have chosen themselves, and the best way to avoid this was to marry the heir at least as young as was reasonable. By Queen Elizabeth's time wardships were usually sold to relatives of the child so this became less of a problem, but the problem was always at the back of parents' minds.

The children of well-to-do families generally had less choice in whom they married than those lower down the social scale: Their parents had a much tighter control over them than poorer families had over their children. A girl simply had to have a dowry if she was to marry amongst the wealthier classes; if her father withheld this then she couldn't marry. Younger sons also rarely had wealth of their own, and even the heir to a fortune had no wealth until his father died, unless his father chose to give him an allowance of some kind.

The economics of marriage was not the only pressure on children to marry where their parents directed. Sixteenth-century children, and girls in particular, were very much brought up to obey, and to believe that it was their duty to their parents, and their whole families, to marry the person chosen for them. It would have taken a very strong-minded girl indeed to have refused to follow her parents' wishes. Girls who did refuse the partner offered could find themselves bullied by their parents. In the mid-fifteenth century Elizabeth Paston was badly beaten by her mother, who feared that she was looking at other men while her family were busy trying to arrange a match for her. Whether or not the mother's fears were justified we do not know, but certainly her relative Elizabeth Clare comments that Elizabeth was being beaten 'once or twice a week, sometimes twice in one day, and her head broken in two or three places'.[3]

There was much more at stake when the child of a rich family married than when a poor one did. A marriage was not just the joining of two individuals, but of two whole families. The network of vital friends, relations and contacts that each family had now became open to the other family. It was for this reason that a wealthy family would happily consider marriage into a well-connected but badly-off family. It was not only the snob value of having aristocratic blood that the rich family was buying, but the contacts that the noble family would have, contacts which could lead to good jobs, good marriages and interesting business opportunites for the rest of the family. It was a disaster when one of your children made an unsuitable marriage because of the lost opportunity for advancement for the family, and because the unsuitable marriage partner would bring with them a network of friends and relations all hoping to gain from the marriage.

In the lower ranks there was much more freedom of choice, as parents had little or nothing to leave their children and so had little hold over them. On the other hand, a poor girl stood a chance of never being able to afford to marry, or of being deserted by her husband if times became really hard.

Marriage was above all a business arrangement, and the choice of partner always began by finding out how much money the family had, and with a discussion around the financial matters. How much the bride's dowry was to be and how and when it was to be paid was usually the first question. Thoughts about the compatibility of the couple often came second. Existing records of marriage negotiations often sound more like the buying and selling of some commodity, such as wool or wine, to the modern reader, than the arranging of a marriage. Parents even sometimes specified in their wills whom their children should marry. In 1533 Robert Burdon, a Northamptonshire gentleman, stated in his will the agreement he had already made with Roger Knollys, saying that his eldest son was to marry Knollys's eldest daughter 'at or before the age of nineteen'. If Burdon's eldest son died, then the second son was to marry Knollys's daughter, and if Knollys's daughter died then one of her younger sisters would take her place. Obviously the compatibility of the couple was not as important as the joining of the two families.[4]

The abuses in the arrangement of marriages were evident to many observers at the time. A large number of books giving advice on how to enjoy a good marriage were published towards the end of the century, among them a pamphlet called *Tell Trothes New Yeares Gift*. 'Tell-Troth' is a character who is supposed to tell the truth about everything he sees. The whole pamphlet is about jealousy in marriage and has harsh words to say about marriages which are arranged purely to enhance a family's social standing without any consideration of the compatibility of the couple:

The first course (of jealousy) . . . is a constrained love when as parentes do by compulsion coople two bodies, neither respectinge the joyning of their hartes, nor having any care of the continuance of their welfare, but more regarding the linkinge of wealth and money together, than of love with honesty: will force affection without liking, and cause love with jelosie. For either they marry their children in their infancy, when they are not able to know what love is, or else match them with unequality, joyning burning Summer with kea-cold winter, their daughters of twentye years olde or under with rich cormorants of threescore or upwards. Whereby, either the dislike that growes with yeares of discretion engendereth disloyalty in the one, or the knowledge of the other disability leades him to jealosie.[5]

The sad thing was that women were the ones who fared the worst in an unhappy marriage. Once a woman married, everything she possessed became the husband's property. It would have been very difficult indeed for her to leave him as she lost all rights to be supported by her husband's property (even if it had once been hers) if she left him to live in adultery.

All this suggests that marriage was a terrible burden on Tudor people, but of course things were not as black as they may first appear. Under the Catholic Church virginity had been seen as the highest and most blessed state, a fact which the new Protestant writers violently disagreed with. According to them, marriage was a gift from God, not a second-best state. Forcing a child into a marriage where it could not be happy was not only unkind, but also brought the holy state of matrimony into disrepute. A great many books were published in the sixteenth century on this very subject, books which also go on to give advice on how to have a successful marriage, how to bring up well-behaved children and so forth. They afford the reader a good idea of what the Tudors expected from marriage.

One thought that runs clearly though all the books is that a successful marriage is founded on love. 'Love' of course can mean many different things, but the Tudors mistrusted passionate love, feeling that hot love soon cooled. Many of the passionate love affairs in Shakespeare's plays led to the death of the lovers. The best marriages were those made thoughtfully and carefully, but with consideration to the couple's compatibility as well as to the business arrangements.

Richard Jones's *An Heptameron of Civil Discourses* is a guide to a successful marriage. It takes the form of a set of dialogues between the well-bred inhabitants of an Italian palace. The seven discourses cover everything from the difference between the married and single life, to the 'inconveniences of over loftye and too base love', the problem with that being that 'spannyels and curres hardly live together without snarling'. It is a mixture of lofty theory and practical advice. A couple should have similar religious views, for example, 'for if thyr love be not grafted in theyyr soules, it is like theyre marriage will be insymed with defects of the body.' It is definitely the role of the husband to rule his household, and that of his wife to see his orders carried out, but a good marriage cannot be built without the consent of both partners: 'The office of free choice, is the roote or foundation of marriage, which comforteth onely in the satisfaction of fancie, so where the fancie is not pleased, all the perfections of the world cannot force love, and where the fancie delighteth, many defects are perfected or tolerated among the marryed.'[6]

Given this feeling, many parents were happy to see their child marry someone they were fond of, provided they came from a suitable family. John Paston III certainly was in love with his wife Margery Brews[7] before they married, and their affection for each other played a large part in bringing the marriage about. John and Sabine Johnson certainly were fond of each other before they married. As early as 1466, Thomas Rokes and Thomas Stronor agreed upon a marriage between their two children but the agreement was to be void if the children disagreed when the boy was fourteen and the girl thirteen.[8] Affection was therefore not always seen as unimportant, but that did not mean that the practical business side of marriage would be forgotten.

As soon as a suitable marriage partner had been found, it was time to begin negotiations. These could be very complicated and drawn out, and often fell through because large sums of money were involved. The contracts could be quite complex, as it was not a simple fact of paying the bride's dowry to the husband. The bride had to be supported by her husband's property for the rest of her life, even if he died some years before her.

In the Middle Ages, common law allowed a widow one-third of her husband's property after he died, but by the sixteenth century this arrangement had largely been replaced by a jointure. This was a holding of land which would be held jointly by husband and wife, and after the husband's death, should he die first, by his widow alone. The chief advantage was that it avoided lengthy disputes as to exactly where a widow's income was to come from. The negotiations as to dowry and jointure were often complicated so it was not surprising that projected marriages often came to nothing.

It wasn't only the wealthy who drew up marriage settlements. Endowments were often paid in money, as even a girl from quite a humble background would hope to have been able to save something, however little, to bring into marriage with her. However, the agreement could be paid in goods and services instead. In 1567 the widow Grace Bab promised her daughter twenty nobles in money, a bed, two brazen crocks, two pans, half a dozen pewter vessels and clothes for her wedding. In 1593 a man of Tedburn St Mary in Devon seems to have given his son-in-law the crops from an acre of ground for a set term, bearing the cost of ploughing, sowing and harvesting himself.[9]

If the woman held land and the man did not it could be the man who had the jointure settled on him rather than the other way round. In 1595 John Dashepener of Littlehampton in Devon offered Elinor Blatchford £20 with marriage to his brother Michael plus the ploughing of their land for as long as he lived with them.[10] Assuming that the negotiations were successful, the wedding could then actually take place. The extent of the celebrations depended very much on the finances of the families involved, but the basics of the ceremony were the same for them all.

Tudor brides wore the best clothes they had for their wedding, rather than the white dresses most brides wear today. The ceremony would start with the couple being brought in a procession to the church. Traditionally the vows were exchanged outside the door, where they could be seen, but in the prayer book of Edward VI the vows are to be made in the body of the church. It was at this point that the bride was formally endowed with the land that would be hers after her husband's death. As a token of the marriage the groom would give the bride a ring, which was placed on the fourth finger of the left hand, just like a modern wedding ring. The ring, however, was not necessarily a plain gold band, but could be as grand or as humble as the couple.

If the marriage vows were exchanged outside the church the couple would go inside for the blessing. After the service was over drink would be served in the church, an important symbol of the friendship between the two families. Even the poorest couples tried to afford this. In 1503 the London smith Lewys Mone got married, his bride being so poor that the only dowry she brought with her was an anvil. She wore borrowed clothes for the ceremony but the couple still had wine served in the church after the service and had dinner at his lodgings.[11]

The ceremony was usually followed by a feast at the home of either the bride or groom, but usually that of the bride. The festivities surrounding a wealthy marriage could go on for days, and no expense was spared to delight and impress the guests. The marriage of Lady Frances Howard and the Earl of Somerset, which took place in 1617, was celebrated with an elaborate masque written by Thomas Campion which was performed in the Banqueting Room at Whitehall Palace. Families who could not aspire to such things still put on the best show that they could and saw that a suitable number and quality of favours, such as gloves, were distributed to the guests. The Tudors were always status-conscious, and the wedding festivities not only demonstrated the wealth of the families concerned but also showed the esteem in which the two families held each other. It was not a good idea to start the marriage off on the wrong foot by stinting on the hospitality.

Not all marriages were celebrated so publicly. In theory, the banns were supposed to be called three times in church before the marriage, at a time when a large number of people would be present. If the couple lived in different parishes, then the banns were to be called in both parishes 'and the Curate of thone parish shall not solemnize matrimonie betwixt them, without a certificate of the bannes beeyng thrise asked from the Curate of thother parishe', warns the First Prayer Book of Edward VI.[12] In practice, it does not seem to have been very difficult to marry secretly if you chose. Certainly even the grandest in the land did so if they thought there would be opposition to their choice. Henry VIII married Anne Boleyn secretly at Whitehall Palace, realizing that the marriage was hardly likely to be popular.

Even clandestine marriages were usually witnessed. Sir William Plumpton married secretly in about 1450 but was careful to have a few witnesses, who were able to remember years later that the bride wore red and Sir William green checks. He was trying to keep his second marriage secret from his first wife's family but he still wanted the validity of his new marriage to be beyond reproach.[13]

The reason for the witnesses was that they could prove that the marriage had indeed taken place. This was an important fact at a time when what exactly made a marriage was not clear. Today, a couple will both sign a paper saying that they are married, and will have a marriage certificate to prove it. This was not the case in Tudor England. In 1563 the Council of Trent decreed that a marriage would be void unless performed before a priest and witnesses, but the decree only covered Catholic countries. In England it was 1753 before there was a similar law. A couple could become man and wife by simply promising themselves to each other, whether or not witnesses were present. Such promises could easily be given in the heat of the moment, and not surprisingly there were those who later wished to deny that a marriage had ever taken place. It was then that the witness of someone who had overheard the exchange of promises could become vital. There are several surviving records of cases brought to court. All kinds of people appear as witnesses, from those who happened to be working in the same field, to apprentices who slept in the same room as one of the couple.

Despite the risks, marriages made in this way were perfectly valid if both partners agreed that promises had been exchanged. The most famous example of such a marriage is that of Margery Paston, who contracted a secret marriage with Richard Calle, a man in the Pastons' service. Margery resolutely refused to say that the marriage had not taken place, despite being put under enormous pressure by her family and also by the Bishop of Norwich. As a result the marriage had to be accepted by the family.

Even if the marriage was not a clandestine one, a priest did not have to be present. The words had to be spoken along the lines of those spoken by a Buckinghamshire man in 1521: 'I Robert take thee Agnes to my weddid wiff for better for worsse and thereto I plyght my traught.'[14] But the vows could be made before parents, an apprentice's master, or simply before a group of friends called together for the purpose.

Consummation was what really made a marriage. Child marriages were in theory not legal unless the children gave their consent when the girl was twelve and the boy fourteen, but if the couple had slept together before that time then the marriage was legal. The debate over the annulment of Henry VIII's first marriage to Katherine of Aragon turned on whether or not Katherine had slept with Henry's brother Arthur, who had been her first husband. Katherine maintained stoutly that she had not when Henry chose to believe otherwise. The importance of consummation in making marriage was the reason for the ceremonial bedding of the couple which would take place after the marriage feast.

The bedding ceremony was often very rowdy, with the wedding party playing games as the couple were put to bed. Even the more decorous weddings included the ceremony. The Puritan element which became stronger towards the end of the sixteenth century did not disapprove of sex, merely of sex outside marriage. Sex between married couples was encouraged and couples were warned not to deny each other sex unless there was some strong reason, such as recent childbirth. William Whately did not mince his words: 'How should their matrimony bee other-wise a meanes of preventing whoredome? How should it else be any way helpfull unto them? How should it indeere their affections? How should it be a comfort of their lives? How a furtherance to their better glorifying of God?'[15]

Despite the complications surrounding marriage for women, it would be wrong to see women as always being victims. There were women who did very well indeed out of marriage. Thomasine Bonaventura, a poor girl of a peasant family from Cornwall, had three wealthy London merchant husbands, Thomas Burnaby, Henry Gall and Sir Thomas Percival. Sir Thomas was even wealthy enough to be Lord Mayor of London.[16]

Bess of Hardwicke was another lady who rose through

careful marriage. Her father died when she was only seven, leaving her with only forty marks. She joined the household of Lady Zouche, where she met Robert Barlow, who married her. He died a few months after the wedding leaving Bess all his lands, woods and lead mines. Fourteen years later Bess married Sir William Cavendish, a widower aged about 42, who died ten years later. Bess seems to have taken over his property for herself and their six children. In 1559, two years after Cavendish's death, Bess married Sir William St Lose, who died in 1565 leaving everything to Bess. She then remarried in 1567 or 1568, this time marrying George Talbot, Earl of Shrewsbury, who was one of the richest men in England. Two of Bess's children married two of the Earl's children. In 1590 he died, after years of estrangement from Bess, but his son and heir found that much of the Talbot property remained in Bess's hands.[17]

Whatever the abuses surrounding the arrangement of marriages, both men and women seemed eager enough to marry in the sixteenth century. In the social atmosphere of the time, this was hardly surprising. A woman was brought up to be a wife, to the extent that this was seen as her calling from God. Men, especially the wealthier ones who had lands and businesses to manage, found life difficult if they had no wife to help them. If their partners died, both men and women often remarried with such speed that it seems quite indecent to us regardless of whether their previous marriage had been a success or not.

Certainly remarriage within a year of a partner's death was common. After her first husband's death Lady

Margaret Hoby remarried within a fortnight.[18] Sabine Johnson's sister Christian died in late spring 1545, being much lamented by her husband. Even so he remarried in January 1546, with Sabine Johnson playing a leading role in bringing about the new marriage.[19] Sabine's devotion to her sister did not mean that she expected her brother-in-law to remain single for the rest of his life. Marriage was above all a practical arrangement – men needed someone to keep house and look after the children, and it took a determined woman to make a living for her children by herself. Even a wealthy widow might need a male protector – Lady Hoby married for the third and final time to get help against the efforts of the Earl of Huntingdon to claim some of her land.

It is, of course, quite impossible to say how happily married the Tudors were and if their distinctly down-to-earth view of marriage made them more or less happy in their marriages than we are today. For one thing, happiness is quite impossible to measure and also their expectations of marriage were so different from ours that it is impossible to compare the two. Doubtless there were some miserable marriages, some very happy ones and many somewhere in between, rather like today. Certainly many married people did come to love each other, even if it was after the wedding rather than before. Marriage in any age is very much what you make it.

TWO

CHILDBIRTH

Childbirth was seen as the most important function of a Tudor woman, but that did not mean that all married women were always pregnant. As we have seen, the majority of women married in their middle twenties, and would continue to have children until their late thirties. Lower-class women, who of course formed the majority of the population, seem to have had a child about every two years, which would mean having around seven children at the most. Upper-class women married rather younger, at around the age of twenty and often did have a child every year. As we have more records of the lives of the rich rather than the poor women it is their experiences which colour our thoughts about the period.

In its early stages, for both rich and poor, pregnancy was difficult to diagnose. Medical books of the time give various tests: for example, one entitled *Aristotle's Complete Masterpiece*[1] includes a whole list of symptoms from fullness and milk in the breasts and 'depraved appetites' to the veins under the tongue being of a greenish colour. There was simply no quick and reliable test as we have today. There were numerous cases recorded of women being treated for various illnesses, not realizing they were pregnant. Moriceau in his *Accomplisht Midwife* of 1673 tells of the wife of a counsellor of the (French) court 'who after having been in a course of Physick of six or seven whole months was at length brought to bed of a child.'[2] There are also examples of women thinking they were pregnant when they were not, the most famous being Queen Mary I herself.

Even when you did know that you were pregnant, there was little that could be done in terms of pre-natal care. For most women there would have been no other food available than the food they ate anyway, and not much chance of varying their normal routine when they were pregnant. In any case, dietary advice was based on the humours,[3] and would hardly be approved of today. Fish and milk were both considered too phlegmatic, and salads were also among the foods that were not recommended.

Pregnant women had to be careful to avoid ugly sights and pictures as well as any sudden fright, as these could harm the child. Moriceau records the case of a mother whose baby was born face first, and therefore much bruised. On seeing the child she thought this was because early in her pregnancy 'she fixed her looks very much upon a Blackmoor belonging to the Duke de Guise, who alwaies kept several of them.'[4]

As there was not much that could be done medically to help prevent mishaps, it is not surprising that great faith was put in amulets and certain stones. The most useful was thought to be the aetites or eagle stone, a hollow stone which has a pebble, sand or other material inside it so that it rattles when shaken. This was not only supposed to prevent miscarriage but was also believed to help relieve the pains of childbirth. It was a very ancient talisman, being mentioned by Pliny, Dioscorides and St Isidore, Bishop of Seville in the seventh century, who wrote about the curative and protective powers of various stones. The eagle stone was thought to attract the unborn child rather in the way that a magnet attracts iron, so that wearing one bound to your arm prevented abortion. It was important to remove the stone and place it on the woman's lower abdomen once labour started, or else the child would not be born.[5]

It was evidently a popular talisman; Dr Bargrave, Dean of Christchurch, Canterbury, in the seventeenth century, wrote of an eagle stone bought from an Armenian in Rome that it was so useful that 'my wife can seldom keep it at home, and therefore she hath sewed the strings to the knit purse in which the stone is for the convenience of tying it to the patient on occasion.'[6]

Guillemeau, in his *Childbirth, or The happy Deliverie of Women*, which first appeared in English in 1612 recommended that a woman should wear a gold or steel chain, or else 'a little gad of steele between the two breasts' as this would stop her milk from curdling.[7]

Pregnancy then as now was not always good news. Few women wrote their feelings down but in poor families more than one or two children meant that they could no longer make ends meet. Even those women who were very happy at the thought of a new baby had their fears about the pregnancy and delivery. The upper classes were particularly desperate to produce a male heir, but a surprisingly large number of them did not do so. Patricia Crawford estimates that in the seventeenth century 19 per cent of landed families died childless, either because they never conceived or because all the children they had died.[8] A pregnancy in a well-to-do family must therefore have been good news, but here is a quote from a letter written in 1623, from Lucy, Countess of Bedford, to Jane, Lady Cornwallis, showing just how terrifying the thought of pregnancy could be:

> itt trobels me more to hear how aprehensive you are of a danger itt hath pleased God to carry you so often safely through, and so I doubt not will againe, though you may do yourselfe and yours much harme by those doubtings and ill companions for all persons and worst for us splenetick creatures. Therefore, dear Cornwallis, lett not this melancholy prevale with you to the begetting or nourishing of those mistrusts (wich) will turne more to your hurt than that you feare, which I hope will passe with safety and end to your comfort.[9]

This was Lady Cornwallis's fourth pregnancy, so these fears were not even those of a first-time mother.

There were those to whom pregnancy was a nightmare come true. These were unmarried women to whom pregnancy meant loss of income and no chance to do anything much about it. A woman who had a baby outside of marriage was considered to have shown herself an untrustworthy character, so that finding work afterwards was difficult. Such mothers might well find themselves being supported by their parish, something that the rate-payers hardly regarded with any enthusiasm. There were also very public penances for such unmarried mothers, which had to be carried out on a Sunday, before a full church congregation.

The thought of abortion must have been tempting for such women. Of course, nobody from the time would have admitted either trying to abort their own child, or helping someone else to abort theirs, so the evidence of such things tends to be indirect. Women at the time might well have been more prone to miscarriages than modern women, due to nutritional deficiencies, pelvic deformities resulting from rickets in childhood, or uterine muscles weakened by long labours, so even convenient miscarriages cannot always be assumed to have been brought on deliberately.[10]

The means to bring on abortion were at hand. Women's commonplace books do contain a number of herbal recipes to 'bring on women's courses', 'promote women's terms' or any number of other phrases meaning to bring back their periods. This is an ambiguous phrase, as it could mean a recipe for use by a woman who had stopped having her periods for some reason other than pregnancy, and wished to bring them back with a view to having a baby. Some of these recipes, however, come with the hint that they may cause miscarriage in pregnant women and they usually contain rue or savin, herbs known to bring on contractions, or involve massage, which can have the same effect. Here is an example, from Markham's *The English Housewife*: 'Water of rue drunk in a morning four or five days together, at each time an ounce, purifieth the flowers in women; the same water, drunk in the morning fastings, is good against the griping of the bowles, and, drunk at morning and at night, at each time an ounce, it provoketh the terms in women.'[11]

Most pregnancies led to a birth, and the rituals surrounding it. Today we tend to regard childbirth as a medical event, a time to be near skilled doctors and nurses, whereas in the sixteenth century it was much more of a social event, a time when a woman wanted to be surrounded by her female friends and relations.[12] The rituals were centred on giving the woman female support, and on allowing her to drop out of normal society for as long as her circumstances allowed and her state of health demanded.

The first part of the ceremony was 'taking your chamber'. This meant retiring, about four to six weeks before the birth, to a specially prepared room, hung with the best hangings the family could afford. The room would be fastened up against fresh air, which was thought harmful at such a time. Details of the preparations made at Greenwich for Anne Boleyn's lying-in survive, and these even included making a 'ffalse rooffe in the quenes bede cham ffor to seyle and hange yt wth clothe of ares and makyng off a cubborde of state with an a place with iii shelves ffor the queens plate to stonde on.'[13] Plate in the sixteenth century was an important status symbol, and a queen would expect to be surrounded by symbols of power as she gave birth to what might be the future heir to the throne.

It wasn't only queens that went to such great lengths. It was common for great ladies to borrow hangings, carpets and other fine decorations for their lying-in. Honor, Lady Lisle, thinking she was pregnant, even tried to make use of the royal wardrobe, not to mention those of all her wealthy contacts,[14] to fit out her chamber. Very wealthy ladies had special pottery for use on such occasions, like the piece in the illustration,which is from an Italian set now in the Fitzwilliam Museum in Cambridge.

When labour began, whether the mother was rich or poor, the various friends – who would have been invited beforehand – would all be sent for, along with the midwife. The women not only kept the mother-to-be company, but also helped the midwife, and made the mother's caudle, a special drink made of spiced wine or ale which was fed to invalids to keep up their strength and spirits.

Much has been written about childbirth at this time, most of it concentrating on some of the horrors that happened when things went wrong. As records are so scarce, nobody can be certain how many women died in childbirth in the sixteenth century, but even in Tudor times most deliveries produced a living child in a matter of hours. This is not to say that the risk to mothers was not much higher than that today. The official UK maternal mortality rate, according to the United Nations,[15] was 0.059 per 1,000 at 1988, as opposed to Schofield's estimate of 14 to 18 per 1,000 before 1750.[16] This, though, was no more than an adult woman's chance of dying from any of the numerous infectious diseases of the sixteenth century, so childbirth was perhaps not as dangerous as most women of the time felt it was. The important point is that the fear of childbirth was very great, as the death rate was high enough for everyone to know someone who had died in childbirth. Considering too that a birth was such a public event, many women must have watched a friend or relative die in childbirth, and a lengthy and painful death it tended to be. No wonder good luck charms to bring a safe and speedy delivery were so common.

Complicated deliveries were indeed not very likely to have a happy outcome. Forceps did not exist at the time, and the only way to attempt to deliver a child that refused to be born was by using metal hooks. This not only killed the child, but tore the mother internally too, leading to infections which could be fatal. Puerperal fever, the cause of Jane Seymour's death, killed a great number of women.

Once delivered, the umbilical cord was tied and cut, the baby washed and then swaddled. Swaddling involved wrapping the new baby in linen bands from head to foot. To us it seems a strange idea, but at the time it was considered essential if the child were to grow up without physical deformity. Nurses even tried to alter their charges' natural looks by swaddling, as this passage from Guillemeau shows:

> Some swathe all the child's body hard to make him have a goodly necke, and to make him seeme the fatter, but this crushing makes his brests and the ribs which are fastened to the back-bone to stand out; so that they are bended, and draw the vertebrae to them, which makes the backe bone to bend and gine out eyther inwardly or outwardly or else to one side and that causeth the childe to be either crump-shouldered, or crook-brested, or else to have one of his shoulders stand further out than the other. . . .[17]

After the birth the mother was confined to bed for three days, with the room kept dark, since labour was believed to weaken the eyesight. At the end of this time came the woman's 'upsitting', after which she remained in her chamber but was no longer confined to bed. (The upsitting was a social occasion, with the mother's female friends being entertained with a meal in the mother's chamber.[18])

It was about this time that the christening would take place, although babies who seemed likely to die were christened at birth by the midwife. Midwives were, in theory at least, licensed by the local bishop in the sixteenth century. Surviving licences show that the midwife had to promise to baptize the child using the correct words, depending on the official religious line of the time when the licence was issued, and was to inform the parish curate of the baptism.[19] Christenings varied enormously according to the social status of the parents. At the top end of society, royal babies were welcomed with all the pomp and ceremony that would attend them for the rest of their lives. When Henry VIII's much longed-for son Edward was christened on 15 October 1537 at Hampton Court, three days after his birth, nearly 400 people were present at the midnight ceremony, whilst on the day of his birth the conduits in London flowed with ale and wine.[20] Even if all babies could not expect a welcome as grand as that enjoyed by Prince Edward, their godparents would still be chosen for them with great care. Godparents were a good way of widening the family's network of contacts, and they seem to have been expected to take an active interest in their godchildren. The Pastons, for example, left various bequests to their godchildren in their wills, while the Church considered godparents as the child's blood relations, so that godparents were amongst those whom one was forbidden to marry.

After the 'upsitting' there would be a further week or so in which the woman would be confined to her chamber, but not confined to bed. The final stage of the confinement consisted of the woman being out of her chamber, but not out of doors. The end of the whole process was marked by a church ceremony known as 'churching'.

The 'churching' ceremony was very short, probably lasting only about ten minutes.The woman would kneel in some convenient part of the church, perhaps in the specific pew some churches had reserved for such a time, while the priest read Psalm 121 (I have lifted up mine iyes unto the hilles, from whennce cummeth my helpe?), the Lord's Prayer and then a short prayer of thanks. The woman then made an offering to the church, and returned the 'crysome' cloth that the child was wrapped in at its baptism.[21]

The ceremony might have been simple, but it was still a matter of some controversy in the sixteenth century. The official church view of the matter had always been that it was a thanksgiving service, but the popular view was that this was a purification ceremony after the 'unclean' process of childbirth. It was customary for a woman to wear a veil, and Puritan opinion, both male and female, felt that this was rather too close not only to Catholic but also to Jewish ceremony. They were very much against the fact that a woman had to give money to the church as part of the ceremony; it was, in their eyes, yet another chance for the priests to make money out of their congregations. The idea of the need for a purification ceremony at all was another factor. To them, childbirth was merely a natural event. Henry Barrow expressed the matter as follows:

> Why are the women held in superstitious opinion that this action is necessary? Why is it a statute and ordinance of their church? An essential part of their worship . . . To conclude, why should such solemn, yea public thanks (to take it at the fairest they can make it) to be given openly in the Church more for the safe deliverance of those women, being (though a singular benefice of God) yet a thing natural, ordinary and common . . .[22]

There were evidently women who felt the complete opposite and who wanted to be churched in the old way. In 1577 an Essex clergyman refused to church three women who were wearing veils, even though they said that they did so 'only for warmth'. The ecclesiastical authorities eventually forced him to church the women, veils and all.[23]

This, then, was the full ritual surrounding childbirth, although of course many women were just not able to drop out of society for a whole month. A study of the Baptismal Register of Preston, Lancashire 1611–1619, unusually records the churching of the parish women. For the 230 baptisms for which churchings are recorded, the gap between the baptism and churching varies from eight to forty-eight days, with most taking place after about thirteen days. The length of a woman's lying-in therefore seems to have varied.[24] Ralph Josselin's wife, Jane, in the seventeenth century lay in for different periods of time, depending on how well she felt.[25]

The mother having recovered, life was still very uncertain for the new baby. Infant mortality was very high – about 13 per cent in the period 1550–99 for children under a year, then about 6 per cent for those between one and four years.[26] There was no real alternative to mother's milk, so a baby who could not be given this for some reason had very little chance of survival. The most influential book on midwifery of the sixteenth century was Richard Jonas's *The Byrth of Mankynd*, published in 1540 and itself a translation of Eucharius Rosslin's *Der Swangern Frawe* of 1513. It recommends that a woman should feed her own child, 'for because that in the mothers bellye it was wonte to the same and feede with it', but few wealthy mothers took his advice. They wanted to get pregnant as many times as possible and suckling their own child helped prevent this. It is no doubt because of this that the book goes into some detail on selecting a wet-nurse.

The child was believed to develop some of the mother's characteristics as it fed from her, so it was very important that the wet-nurse should have the right temperament. Rosslin also describes at some length how she should look, that the mother should ensure that the nurse's 'bulke and breste be of good largenesse' and explains how to test her milk to see that it is suitable. Despite all these instructions the choice of nurse must have been fairly limited, as finding an available woman who had given birth fairly recently cannot have been easy, even in the sixteenth century.

The detail of the early life of Tudor babies is difficult, if not impossible, to work out. For one thing, it was very much a matter which fell into the woman's realm, therefore little was written on the subject. Hints are given in books such as Guillemeau's *The Nursing of Children* which was first published in English in 1612. The baby seems to have lived very much indoors for the first month or so of its life, during which time it would be completely swaddled. After that time its arms would be left free and the nurse would begin to carry it about more, but it was not until it was about eight or nine months old that swaddling would stop completely. There must have been considerable temptation not to change the baby as often as necessary, with all the fiddle of swaddling and unswaddling it every time. Both *The Nursing of Children* and *The Byrth of Mankynd* emphasize the need to change and wash the child frequently, although of course care had to be taken to keep it out of draughts as this was done. Guillemeau gives detailed instructions for this procedure. The doors and windows are to be closed, the nurse is to sit by the fire with a pillow on her lap and to place the child on this as she washes it.[27] These instructions, were, of course, aimed at children of better-off parents, the sort who were Guillemeau's patients and who could afford to buy books. It is a matter of debate as to whether poorer children got the same treatment.

Tudor children were breast-fed for much longer than is common today. The *Byrth of Mankynd* comments that Avicen (a Persian physician who lived 980–1037) recommends breast feeding for two years 'but be it amonge us most commenlye they suck but one yeare'.[28] The child is to be weaned little by little. *The Byrth of Mankynd* recommends giving it bread and sugar to eat at first, but Guillemeau recommends sops of bread (i.e. bread moistened with water or milk) or gruel, then later a chicken leg with most of the flesh removed, so that 'he may the better pull and gnaw it'.[29] Sugar and chicken were both expensive items so were highly unlikely to have been on the menu for most children, who must have been fed the same pottage that the rest of the family lived on.

Guillemeau gives nurses several hints on how to look after the child properly, reminding them, for example, to remember to tie the baby into its cradle so that it didn't fall out as it was rocked. These instructions are reminders that it was almost impossible for a mother to supervise the nurse properly, unless she was living under the mother's roof. It was expensive to have the nurse live in, so most women who chose to have wet-nurses sent their babies out to live in the nurses' home. Babies may well not have been given the same care and attention there as their own mother would have given them, so babies who lived with their own mothers probably had a better chance of survival.

The ceremony surrounding childbirth, whilst having the advantage of giving the woman time off from her usual routine, was rather unhealthy. General medical opinion today is that it is better to get out of bed soon after childbirth and to eat a normal diet. Tudor ladies did themselves no favours by shutting themselves away in stuffy dark rooms and by eating invalid food. Some midwives did more harm than good by trying hasten the birth by stretching the mother and pushing down on her stomach, not realizing that the early stages of the birth ought to be left to happen naturally. The fact that the *Byrth of Mankynde* warns against this practice shows that it must have been common.

Rich women had a tendency to take to their beds during pregnancy and to cosset themselves rather than take reasonable exercise. As it was generally believed that lower-class women gave birth more easily than higher-class ones, there was a social cachet in having a difficult pregnancy and birth, which encouraged the richer women to revel in any problems they had, and perhaps to imagine some difficulties which never existed at all. This seems to have increased as time went on, and by the late seventeenth century various commentators tell women to avoid this habit. R. Barret, in his *A Companion for midwives, childbearing women and nurses*, published in 1699, complains of pregnant women who were 'always stuffing their Guts with slops, having their Chamber Windows adorn'd like an Apothecaries Shop with Pill-Boxes and Gally Pots'.[30]

As we have also seen, richer women usually sent their children out to nurse where they may not have been as well cared for. The net result of all this was that poorer women probably had a better survival rate at childbirth than the richer ones, and more of their children probably survived at least the early part of infancy. It is a relief to know that the poor did better than the rich in at least one respect in the sixteenth century.

THREE

THE EDUCATION OF GIRLS

Until the age of seven, both boys and girls belonged in the female world to the extent that the boys would even wear the same clothes as their sisters. The children's education at this time was informal and was generally the responsibility of the mother. This early education was supposed to include instruction in religion, which was why many writers of the time argued for the education of women. How could a woman instruct her family if she could not study improving books, especially the Bible, for herself? Thomas Becon argues this point in his *The Catechism* published in 1559, when he argues for schools, run by women, to teach young girls:

Is not the woman the creature of God so well as the man? Is not the woman a necessary member of the commonweal? Have not we all our beginning of her? Are we not born, nursed and brought up of a woman? Do not the children for the most part prove even such as the mothers are of whom they come? Can the mothers bring up their children virtuously when they themselves be void of all virtue? Can the nurses instil any goodness into the tender breasts of their nurse children when they themselves have learned none? Can that woman govern her house godly which knoweth not one point of godliness? . . .[1]

These schools were not to be aimed at allowing girls to compete with their brothers, however, but were to be set up on a sound religious basis, so that girls could be taught to be good, obedient and faithful wives, able to raise their children as good Christians.

In the Tudor period education and religion were inextricably bound together. Before the break from Rome the family priest was often also tutor to the children. Many schools were run by the Church, as the parish priest, at least in theory, was supposed to provide free education for the parish children. Chantries, special chapels set up by rich families where masses would be said for the souls of the family dead, often had schools attached. The dissolution of the monastries, and also later of the chantries, led to many schools being refounded on secular lines but religion was still central to a good education. Much of the debate around what exactly children should study was based on what would give them the best foundation in Christian doctrine.

A vital part of education for both sexes in Tudor times was general deportment and good behaviour. In the sixteenth century it was impossible to do well without the favour of those higher up the social ladder, so learning how to be agreeable in company and how to make yourself pleasing and useful to those above you was as important to a sixteenth-century child, male or female, as getting good exam results is to a modern one. For the very wealthy child, the ability to shine socially could lead to a key appointment at court, especially if your social graces could lead to becoming a friend of the monarch.

For wealthy children, this part of their education was quite comprehensive. It included not only a good knowledge of social etiquette but also how to make entertaining conversation, and for the boys how to excel in a range of sports ranging from jousting to tennis. Etiquette books of the time teach young boys in particular even such things as the correct service of dinner to the correct carving of meat. Lower down the social scale this social side of a child's education was not forgotten. A master would be expected not only to teach his apprentice his craft and how to run a business, but also to see that the child learnt good manners.

Behaviour may have been on the curriculum for both sexes, but in all other ways the education of boys and girl became very different once they reached the age of seven. The future roles of the two sexes were so different that this was inevitable. Only the education of the girls will be discussed here.

Before looking at the educational opportunities open to women, we need first to look at the aims of their education. Whether rich or poor, the basic aim of a woman had to be to be capable of looking after her house and family properly. Even wealthy ladies, who may perhaps be learning Latin and other languages, and who had plenty of servants, would be expected to do this. A woman's vocation was above all to see that her husband was comfortable, that his children were fed, clothed, disciplined and educated and that his servants behaved themselves and worked hard.

Sixteenth-century women frequently were involved in their family's business interests but still they were not raised to be the main breadwinner. They were not even allowed to try their skills in some areas. All the professions were closed to them, and all the means of entering them, so that women could not attend either the universities or the Inns of Court. A man's education would simply not have prepared a sixteenth-century woman for the life she was to lead, any more than a woman's education would have prepared a man for his life.

This is not to say that there were not some very well-educated sixteenth-century women, including such famous names as Elizabeth I herself and Thomas More's daughter Margaret. These ladies are so famous simply because they were very much the exception rather than the rule. Their education was also angled differently to that of their male counterparts. An academically educated court lady was brought up to be a jewel of the court, the kind of woman who could hold her own in elegant, witty debate and entertain her husband's guests with suitable grace. She was not educated to compete with her brothers. Even Princess Mary, daughter of Henry VIII and Katherine of Aragon, although she was the heir to the throne for most of her formative years, was not given the practical education in government that she would have had had she been a boy. She was given a very comprehensive education based on the classics, but it was still a court lady's education.

However learned she was, a woman had to remember that she must still obey her husband and, above all, be faithful to him. Castiglione's influential book, *The Book of the Courtier*, first published in Italy in 1528 but not published in English translation until 1561, was very popular in Elizabethan England. It demonstrates very well the position of an educated woman of the time.

The Courtier consists of a number of reported conversations between members of the court of the Duke of Urbino, during which they discuss the attributes necessary to make the perfect courtier, both male and female. The Duke was a rather sickly man, so the court was led by his wife, Elisabetta Gonzaga. In the circumstances it is not surprising that the female courtier is credited with as much intelligence as the male, and at one point Castiglione even puts the following words into the mouth of Giuliano De' Medici: '. . . I say that everything men can understand, women can too and where a man's intellect can penetrate, so along with it can a woman's.'[2]

Even so, the position of women as by nature subservient to men is understood throughout the book, as Giuliano De' Medici also says:

A woman should in no way resemble a man in her ways, manners, words, gestures and bearing. Thus just as it is very fitting that a man should display a certain robust and sturdy manliness, so it is well for a woman to have a certain soft and delicate tenderness, with an air of feminine sweetness in her every moment, which in her going and staying and whatsoever she does, always makes her appear a woman . . .[3]

However clever the woman was, she still had to stay 'soft and delicate' and not think herself a man's equal.

All the books on behaviour written for women gave the same message: a woman must be chaste, silent and obedient. Books which covered subjects such as how to raise your children and how to have a successful marriage all came to this same basic conclusion. Here is a quote from Heinrich Bullinger's *The Christen State of Matrimonye*, written in 1541. It was so popular that it ran into at least nine editions before 1575; so many women must have read it. Parents were to be sure that their daughters

avoyd all unhonest lovers and occasyons of the same, as unhonest daunsynge, wanton communicacion, coommary wythe rybaldes and fthy speachese, teache them to averte thyr sight and sences from all such unconveniences, let them avoyd yollenes, be occupied wither doing some profitable thyng for your family, or elles readynge some godly book, let them not reade bokes of fables, of fond lyght love, but call upon God to have pure hartes and chaste, that they might cleve only to thyr spouse.[4]

Not every writer of the time allowed women such intellectual credibility as Castiglione either. The exact nature of woman was a matter of some debate at the time, as was the effect of education upon women. The principal aim of all women was definitely seen to be wives and mothers; if learning detracted from that, then it was not to be permitted. Those who wanted to see women educated, however, like Thomas Becon quoted above, argued that it would make them better wives and mothers.

Even those intellectuals who had a reputation for supporting women's academic education seem very narrow in their ideas today. J.L. Vives, tutor to Princess Mary, wrote a book called *The Instruction of a Christian Woman* which was published in 1532. Although he was certainly in favour of education for women, he believed that a woman's reading should be strictly limited, and should not include anything but serious moral writings, and certainly no romances. He even thought that a girl should not dance or attend tournaments – something that would have been impossible for a courtly lady.

Dancing and music were, despite what Vives and others may have thought, essential components of a wealthy girl's education. It was a very popular entertainment for all classes, particularly as it was the only time that young ladies and gentlemen could be close to each other without a chaperone. It was for this reason, of course, that many of the moral writers of the time thought it such an unsuitable occupation for a young girl, but in practice you simply could not move in polite circles without being able to dance occasionally. It was also a very good way of getting attention at court, as a graceful dancer might well catch the eye of a wealthy and influential husband. A family did not go to the trouble and expense of getting a daughter a place at court to have her hide herself away in a corner with a book. She was there to further the interests of her family by making sure she was liked by the right people. Dancing was definitely on the curriculum for the court lady, and must have been taught to most women since Tudors of all classes were such great lovers of the dance. The very fact that parents are told so often not to let their daughters dance suggests that it must have been common even for unmarried girls to join in the fun.

Shining at dancing was one thing, but showing too much academic ability was another. Those women who were academically well educated had to be careful how they used their learning. No work of fiction written by a woman has survived from the time, and there were no popular women authors even in areas where woman's expertise was the greatest – in the writing of household manuals or of needlework books. This was partly because writing for publication was considered not quite the proper thing, even for male authors; but also because it wasn't a woman's place to express opinions in public. The only works that women were allowed to publish were translations of religious works written by others; although even in this area women had to be careful to appear humbly dismissive of their abilities. The four daughters of Anthony Cooke, Mildred, Anne, Elizabeth and Katherine, demonstrate this fact. Between them they translated a number of religious works. In the prefaces to these works, the women are presented as modestly publishing almost against their wills, but a study of their private correspondence, such as exists, suggests that these well-educated women were forceful characters who expected their opinions to be taken seriously, even by the highest in the land. Women simply had to put on a public face of modesty.[5]

How then were wealthy girls educated? Like their brothers, young girls were often sent away from home to live in another household. This was not proof that Tudor parents did not care about their children, but quite the reverse. The Tudors firmly believed that children worked best, and therefore learnt best, outside of their families. In large households there were often several children from different families sharing tutors and attending the lord and lady of the house, so that the children could make the right contacts at an early age, rather like attending the 'right' public school today. It is interesting that even Henry VIII himself remained remarkably faithful to the circle of young boys that he grew up with, such as Sir Francis Bryan, and many remained his companions for years. The children were in any case not usually sent away until their early teens, so it was not a case of sending them away as small children.

Once placed in a household a young girl would attend the lady of the house and learn by watching her how to behave in polite society. Other skills she would learn must have depended on the lady herself, and on the sort of social circles she moved in. The plum job for a young girl was to be maid of honour to a grand lady and, of course, the best lady to serve was the Queen herself. Such a position improved a girl's marriage prospects considerably. First of all, she would be displayed to all the most eligible men in the country, men who would be particularly happy to marry a young girl who had the Queen's favour. A position in attendance on the Queen also gave a girl the chance to ask for favours and drop the right hints to help her family's friends and relatives.

An example of the kind of influence that women

attending the Queen could have is found in the Lisle letters. Lady Lisle spent some time trying to get two of her daughters by her first marriage, Anne and Katharine Basset, appointed as maids of honour to the Queen. The time when their chance came is reported by John Hussee, the Lisles' servant, in a letter:

> Madam, upon Thursday last, the Queen being at dinner, by Lady Rutland and my Lady Sussex being waiters on her Grace chanced, eating of the quails, to common of your ladyship and of your daughters; so that such communication was uttered by the said ij ladies that her Grace may grant to have one of your daughters; and the matter is thus concluded that your ladyship shall send them both over . . .[6]

The quails mentioned had been a gift from the Lisles to the Queen. The end result of all this was that Anne was taken on as maid of honour, a post she held for some years even though the queens she served changed. Katharine never became a royal maid of honour although she was very happy for some years in the service of Lady Rutland – and all because the right ladies had dropped the right hints in the royal ear, and because the girls' mother had thoughtfully provided quails for the Queen's table.

Middle-class girls could not aspire to such heights as the Basset girls. Samuel Van Meteren, an Antwerp merchant who travelled through England in 1575, commented on the freedom that married women enjoyed in England, but said that unmarried girls were kept more strictly than those in the Low Countries.[7]

Some girls were apprenticed,[8] but most seem to have been taught at home by their mothers, or attended elementary schools with their brothers where they would learn to read and write in English. Girls at this level would not aspire to learning Latin or Greek. Even those who went to school would be taught the most important things by their mothers – how to look after the house, bring up their children, and supervise the servants. It also seems that many of them could read, even if they could not write.

Today reading and writing are taught at the same time, so we assume that those who cannot write cannot read. In fact, learning to read is much easier than learning to write and so it is quite possible to be able to read, but not write. This seems to have been the case with many sixteenth-century women. It is of course impossible to know exactly what percentage of women could do either but using the records of the ecclesiastical courts for the years 1580–1640, David Cressy suggests that about 90 per cent of London women and 95 per cent of other women could not write.[9] Certainly there were books produced for a female audience at the time, and a study of these gives some clues as to what a midde-class girl would be taught. The books available to her included a large number of books on good behaviour, especially on how a good wife should behave. There were also books on practical skills such as needlework, music, housekeeping and so forth, suggesting that she would have little time to be idle.

Many of the merchant wives must also have learnt to write as it would have been such a useful skill for them. Many merchants spent a great deal of time away from home on business and often they could trust their wives with information which they would hesitate to give to an employee. Many of them also simply wanted to keep in touch with home, like John Johnson, whose wife Sabine was perfectly capable of writing to him as her frequent letters, still in existence, show.[10]

Lower down the scale a girl's education would consist simply of learning the many skills of a housewife. If her parents needed her labour, she would then stay at home until she married, but if not she would be sent away to work for another family as some kind of servant. This was often her best chance. Servants were given their food and lodging and often she would be better fed and housed as a servant than she would be at home. Masters often helped to provide a dowry for a servant who wished to marry, something that a poor father may have been unable to provide.

The one set of skills common to all classes of women were those involved in keeping house. Even if they received very little academic education, all women had to be able to see their families fed, clothed and, if possible, in good health. These skills are usually dismissed by historians as being of no account, suggesting that the inferior education given to women left them unable to do anything very much. This is more a reflection of the low status that housekeeping has always had than a true estimate of the women's abilities.

In the sixteenth century, nobody was brought up to be idle and even wealthy ladies were far from being mere ornaments for their husbands. Their education may not have allowed them to become doctors or lawyers, or to read the classics in the original, but they were still formidable managers, showing a range of skills that would impress even the modern world. The glimpses we have into the lives of some of the women of the time show this range of skills. As representatives of the wealthy women, let us take Lady Margaret Hoby and Grace Sherrington.

Lady Margaret was the earliest known English woman diarist. In her diary she is more concerned with the state of her soul than anything else, but she still mentions many of the duties that she and her servants performed – everything from weighing wool to mixing wax lights and oil, taking her bees and having her honey put in order. She also concerns herself with the business side of running the estates, as she mentions having discussions about buying a farm with a Thomas Adeson, spending evenings reading papers and having numerous discussions about business with Lord Hoby, who seems to have accepted the active part she played. There are numerous references to her being out in the fields, supervising the men's work, so she too must have had a considerable practical knowledge of farming.[11]

Grace Sherrington, who later became Lady Mildmay, left a reminiscence of her early years which gives important information on how a well-bred girl was brought up. Grace was brought up in her parents' house, Laycock Abbey in Wiltshire. She had a governess, a niece of her father's called Mistress Hamblyn, who was much loved by Grace. Grace was never allowed to be idle, but spent her time learning how to cast accounts, how to write a good letter and learning about medicine both from herbals and directly from Mistress Hamblyn. Evidently she learnt well as once she was settled on her husband's estate she spent her time helping the sick and needy, using her knowledge of medicine and surgery (as there was no doctor nearby), designing her own needlework patterns, practising her lute, doing confectionery, and even working out a kind of poor relief system for those living on her estates. She wrote down very detailed instructions for her ten indoor staff, who were no more allowed to be idle than Grace herself was. If Grace was ever exposed to the classical authors, even in translation, she makes no mention of it, but her education could hardly be described as lacking. Certainly it fitted her very well indeed for her role in life and made her a very capable woman.[12]

Lower down the scale were the merchants' wives, such as Sabine Johnson. Sabine shows the same practical knowledge of her estates as Lady Hoby, and is very much involved in the business side of the sheep shearing, for example. She writes to her husband, John:

This shall be to certify you that this day your woolwinders have made an end of winding your wools, and I have reckoned with them. They have wound you 77 sack and 10 tod, and packed 27 cloths. Their winding comes to £4 15s 8d, and their packing 27s so is in all £9 2s 8d, of the which I have given them 40s; the rest my brother must reckon with Dunkerley and pay him . . .[13]

This, of course, came on top of all the day-to-day running of the house, the management of the servants and so on.

The letters that the Johnson family exchange mention several ladies that not only run houses but also businesses, and often quite large businesses at that. They are discussed in more depth in Chapter Seven, but it does show that women's education, although not academic, was deeply practical.

A glance at some of the practical handbooks of the time also gives a good idea of the range of activities that a girl would have to learn to do before she could be considered fit for the responsibilities of marriage. Markham's *The English Housewife*, for example, is described as 'containing the inward and outward virtues which ought to be in a complete woman; as her skill in physic, cookery, banqueting-stuff, distillation, perfumes, wool, hemp, flax, dairies, brewing, baking and all other things belonging to a household.'[14] This, judging by the examples of real women cited above, is not even a full list. There was also the poultry yard, the bees, not to mention any business interests they might have to see to, and the entertaining of guests.

A sixteenth-century woman was often very well educated indeed, but educated in the practical skills she would need to run house and home. There were some women, like the Cooke sisters, who were academically educated but they were the exception, and they had to be careful how they used their knowledge, at least in public. It would be the nineteenth century before women had any chance at all of an education that would allow them to compete with men in any of the professions.

FOUR

HOUSEWORK

There is a general belief that standards of hygiene in the sixteenth century were appallingly low. Tour guides seem to revel in telling stories of how people only washed once a year, and how they never changed their underwear. The Tudors would have been as horrified by these standards of cleanliness as we are today.

'Clean' is a relative word even today, with one person's 'clean' being another person's 'dirty'. Certainly Tudor towns were not clean places, and London in particular suffered due to the sheer size of the problem of disposing of the sewage and rubbish of so many people. This is not to say, however, that most people did not try to keep themselves and their houses as clean as they could, given the limited technology of the period.

The Tudors washed themselves more often than we give them credit for. Royalty did have permanent, plumbed-in bathrooms, like the ones Henry VIII had built at Hampton Court and Whitehall.[1] These magnificent bathrooms were great luxuries, but bathing for most people meant having to fill a wooden tub with water – not something they would bother to do every day. However, there was nothing to stop them washing themselves every day, even if they didn't have a bath, and the fact that there was an interest in personal cleanliness shows through in the recipes in household instruction manuals.

Sir Hugh Plat, in his *Delightes for Ladies*, gives a recipe for 'a delicate washing ball'.[2] Basically, it gives directions for scenting toilet soap, or 'castill sope' as Sir Hugh calls it. Castille soap was expensive, imported toilet soap, made with olive oil rather than the animal fat used in laundry soap. This is the sort of thing a wealthy lady would use for her daily wash.

Recipes for 'hand or washing waters' also abound in the household manuals. A household manual written in the fourteenth century gives directions for preparing washing water, suggesting sage, marjoram, camomile, rosemary and orange peel as possible ingredients.[3] Sir Hugh even gives directions for making one which is 'very cheap', with an eye to household economy.[4] The Tudors never sat down to eat without washing their hands first, and, as they ate with their fingers, never finished a meal without washing either. Washing water would also be brought around during courses, as you hardly wanted the taste of previous dishes on your fingers when you were about to start on something new. These delicate waters would have been used at meal times, but could also be used for your daily wash if you had the money to afford to use them in this way.

Much emphasis is often placed on the number of recipes for perfumes of various kinds that appear in household manuals. These scents, it is said, were used to mask how badly everyone smelt. This is not necessarily the case. Scent was an expensive luxury, containing imported luxuries like spices, and was used as a demonstration of wealth. After all, we still use perfume today, although most of us take great care to wash frequently. Where scent was used to hide more unpleasant odour it was more likely to be the clothes than the people themselves that smelt. Before dry cleaning and deodorants it must have been a problem to keep the tight-fitting Tudor fashions smelling sweet, especially in summer. Even so, every effort was made to keep fabrics that couldn't actually be washed as clean as possible.

In certain cases, cleanliness about the household, as well as about the person, was vital. As we will see in Chapter Five, dairies had to be kept spotless or the produce would be tainted. Markham says that the dairy must be so clean 'that a prince's bedchamber must not exceed it'.[5] It was also accepted that there was a link between dirt and disease, although the existence of bacteria was not discovered until the nineteenth century. It was for this reason that Henry VIII ordered that all the rooms in the apartments of his longed-for baby son, the future Edward VI, should be washed down with soap and swept daily, and that everything that came near the child, whether clothing or toys, should be absolutely clean.[6]

It must have been a difficult job to keep an ordinary Tudor house clean. Earth floors were still very common, and obviously these could not be scrubbed. They also tended to be dusty in summer. Everyday objects were also harder to keep in a reasonable state than modern ones are. China and plastic cups and bowls are much easier to keep clean than the wooden ones used by many ordinary Tudors. Higher up the social scale things were a little easier; flagged stone floors and pewter were not so difficult to clean. Even so, the general cleaning was a time-consuming task.

Household manuals and herbals from the time give us an idea of how the ordinary cleaning was done. It would be the eighteenth and nineteenth centuries before proprietary cleaning agents came onto the market to make the housewife's life easier. In the sixteenth century cleaning had to be done with much more basic materials.

The first thing you need before you can start cleaning is some source of water. Piped water supply, although known in the sixteenth century, was very rare. Water is, of course, difficult and heavy to transport so that often it was easier to take your cleaning job to the source of water, rather than the other way round. A whole range of cleaning jobs was therefore often done outside, even in winter. If you were working indoors the facilities were fairly basic. The 'sink' used for washing up in was likely to be a wooden bench holding tubs.[7] There was also the problem of getting rid of waste water. In smaller, ordinary houses there was no convenient plumbed-in drain to empty waste water down, as we enjoy today. A hole or 'sink' in the ground could be used (see plate 13), although it would have to be outside, which would mean carrying the dirty water to the sink. The trees and other plants surrounding the hole would use up the water. It was only later on, as the villages became towns, that this method of getting rid of waste water became unworkable, as too many sinks in too small an area waterlogged the ground and killed the plants.

Having organized her water supply, the housewife could then start work. One of the most basic jobs that needed to be done was scouring. Everything from the vessels used in the dairy to the knives would need scouring, usually with sharp river sand. The plant known as horsetails (*Equisetum telmateia* being its proper botanical name) was also used to scour anything from pewter plates to armour. Gerard notes in his herbal that the plant was also known as 'shave-grasse' or 'Asprella' and that it was 'not unknowne to women, who scoure their pewter and woodden things of the kitchen therewith.'[8] This was such an important cleaning agent that when supplies began to run out in the eighteenth century they were imported from Holland, so that the plants became known as 'Dutch rushes'.

Horsetails, river sand and hot water might deal with most basic cleaning jobs, but they would not help with another problem that every Tudor housewife had to face. Somehow houses had to be kept free from vermin, which included anything from fleas to rats. Household books are full of methods of killing these unwanted visitors, so it was obviously a major problem. It was certainly one which the Goodman of Paris thought about at the end of the fourteenth century.

The Goodman of Paris was a wealthy Frenchman who wrote a housekeeping manual for his new wife, a girl of fifteen, whom he married when he was at least sixty. He covers a variety of topics, from how to keep the servants in order to how to buy a good cabbage, and gives several suggestions for getting rid of vermin. He lists six ways for getting rid of fleas alone. One suggestion is to lay alder leaves on the floor, so that the fleas will be caught on them;[9] another is to take two trenchers (plates made of four-day-old bread), to smear them with glue or turpentine, and to put them out at night with a lighted candle in the middle of each one. The fleas will be attracted by the light, and then will stick on the trenchers. If the fleas find their way into cloth of some kind, the Goodman suggests binding the cloth up tightly in a bag or chest so as to smother the fleas. None of these methods sounds particularly effective. At best they must have reduced the numbers, but certainly would not have got rid of them altogether.

Thomas Tusser suggests a popular remedy of the time, the herb wormwood. He suggests keeping rooms well swept, and strewing them with the herb, for

Where chamber is sweeped and wormwood is strowne,
No flea for his life dare abide to be knowne.[10]

He also suggests wormwood and rue as useful for cleansing rooms from infection.[11]

Flies were evidently as much of a problem in the past as they are today and the Goodman supplies some ingenious ways of trying to get rid of them. One suggestion was to mix milk with a hare's gall and to leave bowls of this mixture around to poison the flies. Another idea was to hang little bunches of fern up, so that the flies settled on them in the evening, and then to throw the fern out. The advice for dealing with rats and mice is much more practical, starting with the advice to have 'a good array of cats'.[12] The next suggestion has a very modern ring, as the Goodman suggests calling in professional rat and mousecatchers. He also suggests the use of traps and poison made from aconite, arsenic, pig's fat, wheat meal and eggs. The ingredients are made into little cakes which are to be baked and nailed down to the floor.[13]

The hardest part of any housewife's round must have been the washing. Certainly anyone who could possibly afford it employed a washerwoman, which was one of the standard jobs for a poor woman of the time. They certainly would have earned their wages as it was a very time-consuming and unpleasant job.

The Tudors were very fussy indeed about the cleanliness of their linen. Everyone, whether rich or poor, wore a linen undergarment called a smock or shirt. The idea was that everything that touched your skin was made of linen, which could be washed. Clean linen was the mark of a respectable person, and of a good, efficient housewife. In his *Heptameron of Civil Discourses*, a book full of advice on how to have a happy marriage, Richard Jones comments that a woman who does not wear good clean linen 'shal neither be prazed of strangers, nor delight her husband'.[14] Anyone who could possibly manage it would have a clean chemise or shirt every day. Wealthy people, who had plentiful supplies of linen, might change several times a day, for example, after taking part in some vigorous sport like tennis, or after coming back from the hunt.

As if that were not enough linen to cope with, there were also sheets and tablecloths to be laundered. These larger items would often be cleaned by a process known as 'bucking'. A 'buck tub' was a large tub, rather like half a barrel, which stood up on a stand that raised it about a foot from the ground. It had a tap set about an inch above the bottom. A shallow wooden tub was placed under the tap. Filling the bucking tub (or 'laying the buck') was quite a skilled task, as the linen had to be folded and set in such a way that the water poured in at the top would run through all the linen, and so that dirty water would not be caught up in the material and so leave a dirty mark. Sticks were placed between the bundles of linen so that the water could pass through freely, as shown in the diagram.[15]

Once the tub was full of linen, ley would be poured into the barrel. Ley was a strong alkaline solution made in a variety of ways. Sometimes it was made by making water pass through clean wood ashes, but it was also sometimes made from the ashes of dried ferns. In the late seventeenth century Celia Fiennes noted that in Cannock Wood in Staffordshire there was a whole industry which involved half-drying ferns, and then burning these to ashes in pots. The ashes were then made into balls, which were used for washing and scouring.[16] The ley could be used hot or cold, but after the linen had been left to soak for a while the ley would be let out through the tap at the bottom of the tub. The linen would then be turned and rearranged in the tub so that it was all done evenly. Once the dirt was dissolved or loosened the linen was rinsed in running water, and if necessary also bleached in the sun and wind by laying it on the ground or over a bush, and wetting it repeatedly.

Soap could also be used on the wash. It was made by

boiling fat up with lye. It could be made at home, but could also be bought ready made. Soap-boiling was quite a large-scale industry so that many people must have preferred not to make it. Sixteenth-century laundry soap was rather different to the hard blocks of laundry soap that we may be familiar with. It had a jelly-like consistency and was known as 'black soap' as it did appear black while stored in a barrel or pot of some kind. It was the best way of doing the washing, being rather more kind to the linen than other methods. The wealthiest in the sixteenth century wore very fine linen, so fine that you could almost see through it. This delicate fabric must have been washed with soap, as it would never have taken the wear and tear of bucking or being slapped on rocks by a river. Certainly Henry VIII's laundress used soap as it is mentioned in the royal financial accounts. The King's laundress Anne Harris was to wash the table cloths and towels, and provide herbs to keep the drapery sweet. She was paid £10 a year, which was a good salary, but it is stated quite specifically that she must provide her own soap.[17]

After the linen had been washed it could be bleached. Linen is a greyish-cream colour when it is first woven, and only becomes white through repeated bleaching. If you could afford to go to the extra expense of buying your linen ready-bleached it showed your wealth. Everyone therefore wanted their linen to be as white as possible, so that long before advertising women were encouraged to get their wash 'whiter than white'.

In the sixteenth century tubs used for bleaching seem to still have been made of wood, as they were in the Middle Ages. The bleaching process would have been rather like the bucking process described above. It was only when metal vats became common in the seventeenth century that bleaching began to involve boiling up the linen. Bleach itself could be fairly unpleasant. In the sixteenth century human urine was still being used, as it had been for centuries. It was a very cheap source of ammonia and privies sometimes had a special tub set aside purely to collect it.[18] The urine was usually added to lye. It must have been a relief to laundresses when lime replaced urine in the seventeenth century.

Drying the wash was quite a problem. It was usual to dry clothes by spreading them on the ground or by putting them over a bush or hedge, as can be seen in many illustrations of the time. In the winter it was a case of doing the best job you could. It was bad enough drying something simple, like a pair of sheets, but drying the complicated ruffs and ruffles associated with Elizabethan dressing was even more difficult. Ruffs had to be dried over bone and wood sticks until steel rods became available. The steel rods were a great advance as they could be heated and used like an iron.[19]

Some articles would need to be starched before they could be ironed. According to John Stow's *Annals*[20] this art was first taught in England by an enterprising Dutch woman called Dinghen van den Plass, who came to London as a refugee in 1564. Apparently the ladies of London, much impressed by Mistress van den Plass's skills, began to make their ruffs of finer and finer fabrics to test her skills, until it was set that 'shortly they would make ruffes of a spiders' Webbe.' According to Stow, the ladies of London were prepared to spend large sums of money, 'foure or five pound', in order to have their daughters instructed in the art of starching by this clever businesswoman. Unfortunately there is no way of checking the truth of this tale but it does suggest that starching was quite a new process in England at the time.

Not everyone approved of this strange new process. Philip Stubbes in his *Anatomie of Abuses*, published in 1583, had strong words to say about starch. Stubbes seems to have disapproved of many things, but he particularly hated the extravagant fashions of his day which, of course, included ruffs. 'The devil, as he in the fulnesse of his malice, first invented these greate ruffes . . .' he comments. Starch is seen as an instrument of the devil, allowing this demonic fashion to continue. Obviously Mistress van den Plass's skills weren't appreciated everywhere![21]

Stubbs' opinion did nothing to change fashion, and ruffs went on being worn into the seventeenth century. Starch remained in demand and in these early days was also often made from cereals. This meant that in hard times starch took up valuable corn that could have been made into bread. By the seventeenth century the government made use of this fact: it gave them an excuse to ban starch production in England, and to put a hefty import duty on it. In fact, home production never seems to have stopped entirely, but to have fluctuated according to the price starch was fetching at any one time. In practice many people seem to have made their own starch. One way was to use the plant known as cuckoopint. Gerard had this to say about it: 'The most pure white starch is made from it (the root) but it is most hurtful to the hands of the laundress, as it blistereth and maketh the hands rugged and withall smarting.'[22] According to Dorothy Hartley this starch was used to stiffen fine lace. As starching was done using hot water it must have been bad for the laundress's hands.

A further complication to doing the laundry was that rich Tudors loved to embroider their shirts, usually with silk but also sometimes with gold and silver thread. This could be a problem on a garment which needed frequent washing. Fortunately it was one that could be got around, with care. A little book full of instructions for the care of fabrics (amongst other things) survives from the sixteenth century. It was published in 1583 and is a goldmine of information.[23] The book says that a new shirt should have the collar, ruffles and silk (embroidery) laid in warm urine for about half an hour, after which the shirt should be boiled in very hot water or in 'licar' (ley), after which it was said not to stain.[24]

Washing might have been a hard job, but at least it kept linen in good order. The problem was what to do with other fabrics that the housewife had to deal with. Outer garments and blankets were made of wool, which was obviously difficult to launder. Blankets were washed from time to time, but then it hardly mattered if they went out of shape. Clothes were obviously a different matter.

It was a difficult enough problem at the lower end of society but in richer households the problem of looking after fabrics other than linen was far more complicated. A wealthy person's wardrobe would include luxurious fabrics like fine silk, velvet and possibly even cloth of gold. There were also large quantities of fine cloth that were used as wall hangings, all of which had to be kept in good condition. There would also be a great number of furs to deal with, as they were not only common as lining for winter garments and trim for sleeves but were also used for coverlets. Before modern dry cleaning, this was all quite a headache.

Woollen clothes were brushed weekly with a soft brush, and were shaken out regularly if stored away to make sure that the moths were kept out. In his *Book of Nurture* John Russell advises: 'Never let woollen cloths or furs go a sevennight without being brushed or shaken for moths be always ready to alight in them and engender; so always keep an eye on drapery and skinnery.'[25] He also warns against excessive brushing, however, reminding the reader that this will quickly wear wool out.

Moths were a great danger for stored clothes. The Goodman of Paris gives numerous instructions on avoiding moth damage. The worst time for it was the spring, so it was at that time of year that furs and cloth alike were to be hung outside. However, care had to be taken to do this only when the weather was dry, as folding everything up and putting it away damp could increase the problem. After being hung out, the cloth was to be shaken to get rid of most of the dust and then beaten with dry rods to clean it.[26]

There were also various herbs which were supposed to keep the moths out of clothes. One source suggests putting powdered dried orange peel mixed with powdered and dried elecompane roots amongst stored clothes. 'Wormwood or lavender small prevayleth', Mascall adds, suggesting that he had found these two familiar remedies to be less than helpful.[27]

Any furs that had grown hard through being damp were to be sprinkled with wine (the Goodman says to do this by squirting water out of the mouth), left to dry and then rubbed until they were soft again. If the fur was attached to a garment it had to be removed first.[28]

Getting stains out of fine fabric was obviously a nightmare. Dyes at the time were nowhere near as fast as modern ones and it was easy to make the problem worse if you did the wrong thing. There is plenty of advice for getting various stains out of all types of fabric, but the very fact that so many alternative ways of treating stains are given suggests that getting the marks out was a rather 'hit or miss' affair. Stain removal could also be quite a complicated business. An example of one instruction is found in John Partridge's *Treasury of Commodious Conceites*. It is supposed to remove spots from cloth of gold and velvet: 'Take raw red arsenick (and) Mertum Cudum,[29] of each of them a like much and when they be well braied poure some fair water upon them, and putting the hearb cinkfoyle to it seethe it into half and then let it coole, and set it in the sun two houres, then washe your cloth in it and let it dry in the sun.'[30]

Fortunately not all the instructions sound so alarming. One of the ways given for cleaning velvet and scarlet (very high quality wool) in *A Profitable Book Declaring Dyvers Approved Remedies* uses a common sixteenth-century detergent, soapwort, or *saponaria officinalis*. Gerard states that this was also used to soften bathwater and as a toilet soap. The instructions in the *Profitable Book* say to beat the soapwort until soft, and then to remove the juice. The juice is then put on the spots, and left one hour in summer and four in winter. The spots are then washed with clean water, and the juice is reapplied. Finally the soapwort is washed out using lukewarm water. Evidently this was one of the more reliable methods of stain removal as the author adds proudly at the end of the instructions, 'for this way is proved by experience to be true.'[31]

Ordinary soap could also be used with care on fine fabrics. The author of the *Profitable Book Declaring Dyvers Approved Remedies* suggests washing both silk and gold (this could be either cloth of gold or gold embroidery) by heating water then adding soap. The soap is then allowed to melt, and the water is left to cool until it is almost cold. The garments are then washed in the water, and dried with dry cloths laid between the layers.[32]

Grease, then as now, seems to have been a particular problem. The fact that it was so hard to remove explains why Tudor table manners were so much better than is often suggested by films and television. Nobody wanted to come away from the table with their clothes ruined, especially when they were wearing their court best. Even the most delicate of eaters must have had the odd accident, however, and it was then that some method had to be found to put the damage right. John Partridge suggested using the water in which peas had been soaked[33] while the *Profitable Book* suggested applying Castille soap with a clean feather,[34] or else using fuller's earth.[35]

The remedies that survive from the sixteenth century are most likely only a selection of the stain removal techniques that were used at the time. No doubt every housewife had her own favourite methods and tips. What is obvious is that it was all a very complicated business. Cleanliness was definitely seen as a virtue in the sixteenth century, but it was unwise to go to extremes. Sixteenth-century cleaning methods could be hard on household utensils, and too much cleaning could damage them. Here is a warning from Thomas Tusser:

No scouring for pride
Spare kettle whole side
Though scouring be needful, yet scouring too much
Is pride without profit, and robbeth thine hutch.[36]

I expect most housewives were happy enough to take this advice.

FIVE

FOOD AND DRINK

To speak then of the outward and active knowledges which belong to our English housewife, I hold the first and most principal to be a perfect skill and knowledge in cookery, together with all the secrets belonging to the same, because it is a duty really belonging to a woman; and she that is utterly ignorant therein may not by the laws of strict justice challenge the freedom of marriage, because indeed she can then but perform half her vow, for that she may love and obey, but she cannot serve and keep him with that true duty which is ever expected.

It is with these forthright words that Gervase Markham opens the section on cookery in *The English Housewife.* This was first published in 1615, just after the end of the Tudor period, but Markham was born in 1558 and was very much a child of the Tudor era. In terms of his day he was quite right. Keeping the family fed was the major part of a Tudor woman's work.

The women themselves would have agreed with this view. A good example of this can be found amongst the surviving letters of the Johnson family, who were well-to-do merchants in the mid-sixteenth century. In 1545 they took a new apprentice, by the name of Pratt, who was sent to live at the Johnson's home at Glapthorne Manor in Northamptonshire. Unfortunately, young Mr Pratt was not pleased with his lot and soon his mother was rushing to see John Johnson in London. After the interview John wrote to his wife Sabine who was at Glapthorne:

Your young gentleman, Master Pratt, hath complained by his letter to his mother that he lacketh both meat and drink, as well as his breakfasts, as also at meals not sufficient. All your menservants have been of counsel with him, for they be of no less opinion, declaring that your bread is not good enough for dogs, and drink so evil that they cannot drink it but are fain when they go into the town to drink to their dinners. If ye know they complain with cause, I pray you see it amended: if they complain without cause, let them seek new masters and boarding.

Sabine's reply, after questioning the servants, was as follows:

As for Master Pratt's complaint, I can find nobody in fault but himself, and he doth deny that he did write any such things but lack of meat and drink. If three meals a day and four in summer be not sufficient, I would his mother had him, that she might feed him every hour. I will have all my house to say with me that he had his breakfast, his dinner and his supper all well eaten.[1]

Just to prove her point, she sent a batch of bread she had made by the carrier who was to take the letter, which she intended to be given to Master Pratt's mother as proof of her abilities. Tactfully, John never passed the bread on, but this shows how important a woman's skill in the kitchen was to her. Sabine Johnson would allow no gossip in this respect. Even important ladies, such as Lady Elinor Fettiplace, part of whose receipt book has been published,[2] showed a very personal interest in cookery. Lady Fettiplace not only recorded many recipes in her own hand, but also annotated her book with little notes, just as many keen cooks annotate favourite recipe books today. 'Two or three spoonfuls of water' is changed to 'four' and there is advice on how to improve a dull sauce recipe: 'You most put som whit win in to the gravi with the venygar.'

For the majority of the population food was very simple. Bread and pottage were the order of the day. Pottage was rather like porridge, with vegetables and, if you were lucky, meat. Most people could not afford to eat meat every day, so the nourishment came from the grain, usually oats or barley. At the lowest end of the scale, therefore, actual cooking would not take long. Pottage is not only a useful meal for making a little go a long way, it is also very easy to cook. Once the ingredients were set to cook in a cauldron over the fire they only needed the occasional stir, so the cooking didn't interfere with other work.

Bread could be more of a problem. It is not particularly time consuming to make, but it could be difficult to cook, as many houses did not have ovens. Ovens were expensive to heat, and had to be built into a brick or stone wall, something that was clearly impossible in tiny labourers' cottages which were usually built of wattle and daub. In towns, where houses tended to be long and narrow, sometimes even the wealthier merchants had no oven, as the houses were not wide enough to accommodate one. You could improvise by turning a pot upside down over the bread and covering it with hot coals, but the usual answer was to pay to use either the baker's oven or the local communal one. Even in London, where there were plenty of bakers who would bake for you at a price, there were also communal bake houses. This was not surprising, considering the amount of bread that had to be cooked. The surviving accounts of great houses suggest that people ate between two and five pounds of bread in a day. Little wonder that at the great meeting of the English and French kings at the Field of the Cloth of Gold in 1520, where some twelve thousand people had to be fed, a huge brick bread oven was built especially for the purpose. It can be seen on the painting made to commemorate the event, which now hangs at Hampton Court.

Bread was more than the staff of life, it was also an indication of your station. At the bottom of the ladder came horse bread, made with dried peas that had been ground up to make flour. Usually this was – as its name suggests – fed to horses, but in famine years the poorest people could find themselves reduced to eating it. The next rung up was maslin bread, which was a mixed grain bread made from wheat and rye, or whatever grain grew best locally. It was a brown bread, and would certainly have sustained you through a day's work. The best bread was, however, fine white bread called manchet.

Today, when the virtues of a high-fibre diet are well publicized, people are often surprised that white bread was so highly valued. There were various reasons for this. First of all, Tudor bread would have been much heavier than most modern bread. English wheat is naturally 'soft', that is to say, it has a low gluten content. It is the gluten in the flour that traps the bubbles of air given off by the yeast which makes it rise. Most bread flour we use today is imported 'strong' flour with a higher gluten content, so that our bread rises better.[3] The brown bread would therefore have been quite hard work on the teeth, making white bread a pleasant proposition. The very fact that brown bread was more sustaining made the wealthier people less keen to eat it. Manchet showed that you had finer food to eat than bread to fill your stomach with – it was an elegant accompaniment to a meal. There was the added bonus that as the flour to make manchet had to be carefully sifted through a fine linen cloth it took a long time to make and was therefore expensive. In an age when it was important to make great display of your wealth it was a useful status symbol.

The hardest work in the kitchen came a little higher up the social ladder. The 'middling sort' of woman, for whom books on 'housewifery' began to be written towards the end of the Tudor period, had more work to do. These women were expected to provide far more than a simple pottage. They wished to live something near the life of the gentry but had only a servant or two to help them in the house. They had to know not only how to cook whatever food was needed, be it meat, fish or game, but also how to serve it as great store was laid by providing an elegant place setting. A good display at meal times was as important as the way you dressed – as was discussed in the Introduction. The family would lose face if the housewife could not present guests with a number of dishes, ranging from plain boiled and roast meats to fancy spiced sauces.

A feast that Markham suggests suitable for a household of this class consists of the following: a shield of brawn (the skin of a boar filled with jellied meat) with mustard, a boiled capon, a piece of boiled beef, a roast chine of beef, a neat's (i.e. calf) tongue roasted, a roast pig, baked chewets (pies made with minced meat), a roast goose, a roast swan, a roast turkey, a roast haunch of venison, a venison pasty, a kid with a pudding in its belly, an olive pie, a couple of capons (Markham doesn't specify how these should be cooked), and finally, a custard or doucet (spice custard pie). This was only to be the basics of the spread, and Markham goes on to say: 'Now to these full dishes may be added sallets, fricasees, quelquechoses, and devised paste, as many dishes more, which make the full service no less than two and thirty dishes, which is as much as can conveniently stand on one table . . .' These 'sallets, fricasees, quelquechoses and devised paste' were the finishing touches which every housewife would take great pride in, but which would take her hours to produce.

'Sallets' could include anything from a very simple vegetable dish such as boiled carrots to a magnificent dish produced only for show, such as the one suggested by Markham himself. This is to be made of carrots carved into the most elaborate shapes, such as birds and wild animals. Certainly as much care was put into the appearance of a sallet as to how it tasted, and flowers were carefully preserved in sugar or vinegar for decorating them when fresh ones were not available. Lady Fettiplace, for example, gives instructions for doing this. The 'fricasees and quelquechoses' were various dishes made in the frying pan, and included pancakes, fritters, and dishes made with meat such as veal toast.

'Devised paste' was in a class all on its own and brings us to the skill that was necessary to all ladies with any pretensions – that of confectionery. In the Middle Ages, when sugar had first been introduced into England, it was considered a medicine. It was thought to be especially helpful for the digestion and so began to be served at the end of grand feasts, usually in the form of candied aniseeds. As women were the doctors for their households, such sugar work naturally fell to them, as sugar was far too expensive to be left to the servants to handle.

By the middle of the Tudor period sugar was relatively cheaper than it had been in the Middle Ages, but it was still not cheap. It cost about 9d a pound in 1547 at a time when a shipwright, a skilled man, was earning about 6d a day. Even by the early seventeenth century, when a mason, another skilled man, was earning 16d to 18d a day, single-refined sugar cost 22d a pound – and that was not the best quality.[4] This made it too expensive for the working classes but cheap enough for the middle classes, and so it was the ideal status symbol. The ability to produce all kinds of confectionery therefore became a sign of breeding and the development of 'banquets' gave women a perfect outlet for their creative skills.

A banquet was not a meal in its own right, but the final course of a feast. Usually the banquet was only attended by a select few, and was often held in a separate room. The serving of sugar went beyond candied aniseeds and became, as the Middle Ages progressed, a whole course of sweet dishes and spiced wine, which, as it was so expensive, was served only to the top table. Medieval diners sat at trestle tables which were cleared as soon as the meal was over. In order to avoid the noise and bustle of this being done, it became usual to serve this course in another room. As time went on, this 'banquet' course was served in separate 'banqueting' houses, which were often built outside in the garden. (Henry VIII had no less than three at Hampton Court.) The food offered consisted of all manner of sweet dishes – candied fruit, marmalade (which was then often made very thick and cut into slices, as it still is in Portugal), sweet wafers, gingerbread, and a whole variety of items made with sugar paste sometimes even including the plates and cups used for this course, which could then be eaten afterwards. The sugar paste used was very like the fondant icing used today in cake decoration, and books from the time describe literally hundreds of different 'deceits' which could be made from it. An egg which breaks open to show a yellow yolk, 'bacon' made from strips of different coloured paste, fruit and walnuts – these are but a few examples.[5]

Cooking was not the housewife's only part in providing food. There were various offices associated with the kitchen which she also supervised. Even women who could not aspire to producing fine sugar work had to know how to keep a dairy, for example. The dairy was especially close to a woman's heart, as by tradition the profits from it belonged to her to do as she liked with.

From April beginning, till Andrew be past,
So long with good housewife, her dairy doth last,
Good milchcow and pasture, good husbands provide
The res'due good housewives know best how to guide.

Ill housewife, unskillful to make her own cheese,
Through trusting of others hath this for her fees,
Her milk pan and cream pot, so slabbered and sost,
That butter is wanting and cheese is half lost.'[6]

Certainly Sabine Johnson took great pride in her cheeses, and sent them not only to merchant friends at the Staple in Calais, but also to her husband and brother-in-law in London. 'They two cheeses that be scraped on the oven I take for the best', she wrote to her husband on one occasion, 'but I would they were better; as so good as I find it in my heart to send to you.'[7]

Butter and cheese were a vital way of preserving milk for the winter. By the eighteenth century many ladies had very pretty ornamental dairies built, in which they played the dairymaid just as Marie Antoinette played at being a shepherdess. As a result, dairying has a rather ladylike image to us, but serious dairying is not for the faint of heart. For one thing, it was well understood even in Tudor times that the dairy must be kept spotless. The taste of dairy produce can easily be tainted, and dirt can also stop some of the processes working. Hours had to be spent scrubbing floors and scalding vessels – Markham recommends the scalding of all the vessels used in the dairy once a day. Much of the other work about the dairy was remarkably heavy too, such as churning butter. Even the lighter task of potting up butter for keeping or selling meant working the salt through the butter with your hands.

Despite the hard work, dairying was well worth the effort. The hard cheese that was made for keeping (and which was rather like modern cheddar) was considered so essential to the poorer people's diet that sailors on the king's ships were issued with 2 lbs of it on three days a week, and 1 lb another day. Soft cheese, which would be matured for a while, but not for as long as hard cheese, was also eaten in large quantities. Curd cheese (green cheese) was a third form of cheese which was not designed for keeping and had to be eaten quickly.[8] The whey, known as 'whig', was not wasted, but drunk.

Cream was used for cooking by the better-off, and had a hundred uses. It was made into luxuries like syllabub; it went into a variety of both sweet and savoury puddings and was made into sauces. The poorer housewife would not have wasted her cream on such luxuries, but would have used it for making butter. The only time she would have eaten cream would have been on special days such as May Day when cakes and cream were served to people coming home from maying.[9]

One vital area of cooking that touched all classes

was the preservation of food. The housewife's life was a constant battle to preserve whatever was in season against the time when it was not. If the more genteel preserves involving expensive sugar were beyond many housewives, they still had the work of salting down meat for the winter. For many families the only meat they ate was that which came from the family pig, which would be killed in autumn before it began to need expensive winter feed. If the pork was salted hot, it took two ounces of salt for each pound of meat, plus another two ounces of saltpetre. If the pork was soaked in brine instead, then the brine had to be strong enough for an egg to float on it. According to my own experiments, that meant using at least five ounces of salt for each pint of water. No wonder salt was treasured.

The salt used for preserving was usually bay salt, so called because it was produced on the Bay of Bourgeneuf, although the same name was used for salt made all along the French Atlantic coast and in northern Spain and Portugal. Home production of salt had not been able to keep up with demand since the beginning of the thirteenth century, and Bay salt made up the difference. It was a dark salt, full of impurities as it was evaporated from sea water. It was preferred as not only did it cost less than the more carefully refined white table salt, but it was also better for preserving. Its coarser texture penetrated the flesh better than the finer salt, which tended to seal the surface of the meat without entering deeply.[10] Either way, salting was not a pleasant task. Rubbing large amounts of salt into meat would certainly have taken its toll on the housewife's hands.

Fortunately housewives usually had only to think of

preserving meat, and not fish. Fish was usually bought in its cheapest form, as dried and salted stockfish. This was imported from Scandinavia, and sometimes even from Russia. It was said to last for up to four years and was very hard when taken out of its barrel. It had to be beaten with a wooden hammer for a full hour before being used, and then soaked in warm water for two hours before being eaten, and it could get very boring. It was usually put in pottage, or boiled and eaten with mustard or butter. In the previous century one schoolboy, fed up with the Lent fish diet, wrote: 'Thou wyll not beleve how wery I am off fyshe, and how moch I desir that flesh were cum in ageyn, for I have ate non other but salt fysh this Lent, and it hat engendyrde so moch flewme within me that it stoppith my pyps and I can unneth speke nother brethe.'[11]

Considering that throughout the sixteenth century fish went on being eaten two days a week, by order of the church, it must have been a relief that fish didn't have to be preserved at home. Wealthy people in any case ate fresh fish all year round. Anyone who owned an estate would have had their own fish ponds to ensure a steady supply. Fresh fish, though, was usually reserved for the family, their guests and more important servants. Lower down the scale the household had to eat stockfish unless they lived very close to the sea where fresh fish could be obtained cheaply.

Fruit and vegetables also had to be preserved. Some, like apples, could be stored in a cool, dry room often set aside for the purpose. Others, such as vital peas and beans, would be dried. This could be done before the fire, or, if you were lucky enough to have an oven, you could make use of the last heat of its firing for this purpose. Herbs, then as now, would be hung in bunches and left to dry.

Pickling was another alternative: this was done either in vinegar or in verjus, both of which were often made at home. Vinegar would be made from strong ale which was left in the sun until it was sour. In continental Europe verjus was made from unripe grapes but in England was usually made from the more freely available crab apple. The crab apples would be left to rot until they were black, and then mashed up in a long trough by beating them with wooden hammers. The resulting mash was then strained through a coarse cloth and put in barrels, together with a dozen handfuls of damask rose leaves for every hogshead of verjus.[12]

The Tudor housewife did not only have to keep her family supplied with food, but also with drink. It was generally acknowledged that sickness came from drinking water, and milk was only considered suitable for the very young or old and the sick. The alternative was to drink ale or beer. In Tudor terms these two drinks were basically the same thing, except that beer was brewed with hops and ale without. Instead, ale was flavoured with various herbs and spices – there were so many different recipes that every housewife seems to have had her own! Ale had been the traditional English drink for centuries, but did not keep as well as beer (the hops act as a preservative) and so was gradually dying out. Beer was especially useful on ships, as voyages were becoming longer so its longer life was vital. It was not everyone who looked favourably on beer, even so. Andrew Boorde, physician to King Henry VIII himself,

wrote in his *Dietary of Health* that he considered ale the
natural drink for the English and that beer was bad for
the health.

The brewing process was similar for both ale and
beer. First the grain, which was usually barley, was
malted. This meant that the grain was dampened, and
left in a warm place until it began to sprout. It was
then roasted to stop it germinating further. This malt
was then added to boiling water which was flavoured
either with herbs and spices (for ale) or hops (for beer).
It was this boiling that made ale and beer safe to drink
even when the water could not be trusted, although of
course the Tudors would not have understood this. The
resulting liquor was then barrelled, and yeast added so
that it fermented.

A Tudor housewife would use her malt three times
if she was making beer. (One of the advantages of
brewing beer rather than ale was that the malt could be
used more than once.) The first time it would be used to
make strong beer. This could be very strong indeed, and
could keep for up to two years. It would be drunk very
much as we drink beer today, as would the weaker
brew that would come from the second use of the malt.
The third use would make small beer, which was very
weak. It was far too weak to get drunk on, and
everyone, from the highest to the lowest, drank this
when they were thirsty. Not surprisingly, it was drunk
in great quantities. Judging from the account books of
the great houses, and from the ration handed out to
the king's sailors, a gallon a day was the norm. Great
houses had specially equipped brewhouses, together
with maltings for making the large amounts of malt this

must have consumed. Even so brewing was such a simple process that it could be done over the household fire. The equipment was fairly cheap and ale and beer could always find a ready market as there was so much demand for the product. It was for this reason that licences to run alehouses were often granted to poor women who had no other means of supporting themselves.

Cider was drunk at this time, but only in areas such as Devon and Herefordshire where great quantities of apples were grown. Its quality was definitely variable at this time and it was not until the eighteenth century that English cider became generally esteemed. At its most basic cider was very rough indeed. Mead was still being made, but was not drunk in large quantities. It was kept for special occasions and even then richer people preferred wine.

Wine was an expensive luxury as it was imported. It was usually bought in bulk rather than in small quantities. Larger households would even buy it by the tun, a large barrel holding 256 gallons. The more expensive wines, the heavy, sweet wines known as Malmsey or Romney, were usually bought in smaller quantities. They came from as far away as Cyprus and cost twice as much as claret, so that they tended to be bought by the butt (usually half the size of a tun).

Both buying and looking after wine was an art. These were the days before corks, when wine scarcely lasted a year. The laying down of wine for future years, and the division of harvests into greater and lesser vintages was not a possibility in the sixteenth century. At this time, the wine trade centred around getting the new vintage home in time for the Christmas market, and getting rid of the previous year's stocks before the new wine came home. Once a barrel had been tapped the air was allowed in and the wine would go off fairly quickly. The problem was how to make it last as long as possible. Vintners, of course, shared this worry and were always looking for ways of passing off bad wine as good. It took a skilled person to detect some of their tricks, and often skilled help was called in when buying wine to help detect fraud. Good wines and bad were often mixed, and vintners were so tempted to let customers taste one wine, and then sell them another that the law required them to leave the doors to their cellars standing open during business hours so that everyone could see exactly what was going on.

The housewife, though, was in a rather different position. What was considered dishonest in a vintner was considered good economy in a housewife. Markham thoughtfully provides a number of hints on how to make off wine palatable. He provides a whole section on the 'ordering, preserving, and helping of all sorts of wine'. The housewife is to add a syrup made of damsons or black bullaces to claret that has lost its colour, and to add apples, or a herb called oak of Jerusalem to foul-tasting wine in order to restore its flavour. These are only two examples from a long list of instructions. Keeping wine was clearly a major headache.

In spite of the hard work of Tudor housewives it is a mistake to think that all food and drink was home cooked and prepared at this time. There were always plenty of cookshops in towns where food could be bought ready made. Food took time to prepare, so an unexpected guest could mean that a trip to the shop was the only quick answer. There was also always a floating population of people who lived in lodgings without cooking facilities – shipwrights and builders, for example, who followed work around the country – who could not cook for themselves. Even the well-off did not have everything made at home. Sabine Johnson bought her spiced comfits ready made. They seem to have cost about a shilling a pound, so were not cheap, but who can blame Sabine? The alternative was to spend three hours over the charcoal-heated chafing dish making them yourself, and even then you had to pay for the sugar. It's good to know that there were at least a few short cuts for the hard-pressed housewife.

SIX

THE HOUSEWIFE AS DOCTOR

To the casual modern reader, Tudor medical books, especially herbals, seem an odd jumble of unlikely ingredients with no particular method behind them. In fact, the cures are logical according to the medical theories of the time, even if a modern doctor would not agree with them.

At the very base of Tudor medicine was the idea of the four humours. This was a very old idea, dating back to ancient Greek doctors, particularly Galen and Hippocrates. The idea was that earth, air, fire and water made up all things. Each of these elements had a corresponding quality: earth was cold and dry, air was hot and moist, fire, hot and dry and water, cold and moist. Imbalance of these elements was what caused disease.

The four humours that went to make up the human body were blood, considered to be hot and moist, red choler, which was hot and dry, black choler, which was cold and dry, and phlegm, which was cold and moist.

The four basic temperaments which were thought to exist depended upon which of these four humours was dominant in each individual. These temperaments were: phlegmatic (cold and moist), choleric (hot and dry), sanguine (hot and moist) and melancholic (cold and dry). If this all sounds rather confusing, the table below should make matters clearer:

Element of Earth	Its Qualities	Corresponding Temperament	Dominant Humour
Air	Hot and moist	Sanguine	Blood
Fire	Hot and dry	Choleric	Red choler
Earth	Cold and dry	Melancholic	Black choler
Water	Cold and moist	Phlegmatic	Phlegm[1]

Studying a patient's looks and habits would tell a doctor what his basic constitution was. Here is an example from Sir Thomas Elyot's *Castel of Helth*, a best-selling health manual of the sixteenth century. Sir Thomas annoyed the medical establishment of the time by writing the book in English, with the aim of providing medical knowledge to those who couldn't read Latin. The following is a list of signs of the 'phlegmatic' temperament: 'Fatesse, quavying and soft, vaynes, narrow; heare much, and plaine; colour, white; sleape, superflous; dreams of thynges watrie, or of fyshe; slownesse, dulnesse in learning; cowardice; pulse slowe and lyttell; digestion weake; spittell white, abundant and thicke; urine grosse, white and pale.'[2]

The appeal of the theory of the four humours becomes obvious from this description. It could be used to explain not only someone's physical makeup but also psychological problems like 'dulnesse in learning'. It was such a wonderful, neat theory that the medical establishment were very unwilling to give it up, even when the more scientific approach to medicine that began in the sixteenth century showed that it could not be true. Medical treatment was centred around restoring the balance of the humours, bearing in mind a person's basic constitution. Everything, including rocks and plants, was considered to be made up of the four elements and to have qualities which could help towards a cure. Here, for example, is how Sir Thomas Elyot describes the qualities of lettuce:

> Among al herbes, none hath so good juice as lettice for some men do suppose, that it maketh abundaunce of bloude al be it not verie pure or perfect, it doth let a hot apetite, and eaten in the evening it provoketh slepe albeit it neithr doth losse (loose) nor bynde the bealye of his owne propretye. It increaseth milke in a womans' brestes but it abateth carnal appetite and much thereof hurteth the eye sight. It is cold and moyst temperately.[3]

Lettuce, being 'cold' was, like other 'cold' herbs ideal for treating 'hot' complaints, such as fevers. Here is an example from one of the cures given in Markham's *The English Housewife*:

Of thirst in fevers
It is to be understood that all fevers of what kind soever they be, and these infectious diseases as the

pestilence, plague and such like, are through the inflammation of the blood, incivilly much subject to drought; so that, should the party drink so much as he desired, neither could his body contain it, nor could the great abundance of drink do other than weaken his stomach, and bring his body to a certain destruction. Wherefore, when any man is so overpressed with desire of drink, you shall give him at convenient times, either posset ale made with cold herbs; as sorrel, purslane, violet leaves, lettuce, spinach and such like. . . .[4]

Certain humours could also change as people aged, or as the seasons changed. For example, the signs of Aries, Leo and Sagittarius were linked with the planet Mars, Fire, the west wind, summer and childhood.

Besides a knowledge of the humours, a Tudor doctor also needed a good knowledge of astrology. The moon was known to control the tides; it was logical that the humours of the body were also controlled by the planets. The stars were thought to dominate the whole of nature to such an extent that outbreaks of plague were even blamed upon their influence, as in the wrong places the stars could bring about infected air. Sir Thomas Elyot explained that 'the causes whereby the ayr is corrupted be specially four: the influence of sundry stars, stagnant waters, carrion and overcrowding.'[5]

The position of the stars was also thought to dominate certain parts of the body to such an extent that it was hardly worth attempting the cure if the astrological signs were not good. Arnold of Villanova, a famous medieval doctor, wrote, 'The planet which acts most on the qualities of a man is the moon. . . . From its phases the crisis of an illness can be foretold and when in conjunction with the constellation Pisces the outlook is always good. The moon's phase can enhance or interfere with a remedy. So it comes that measures which can be taken otherwise would avail nothing. . . .'[6]

Astrology was such a vital part of medicine that at the Sorbonne, and other universities, a Chair of Astrology was combined with that of Medicine. It was so much linked with medicine that publication of astrological charts formed a useful sideline for the well-known doctors of the period. Andrew Boorde was one such doctor. In 1537 he published an *Almanacke and Prognostigation*. The 'astrological man' was also a very common illustration in medical books of the time. An example, now in the British Library, is shown here. Blood-letting was a common cure at the time, believed to help balance the humours. At this time, the fact that blood circulated throughout the body was not understood, and so the place from which the blood was taken was considered vital. The 'astrological man' shows how each part of the body is governed by the stars, so that you could work out the best time to bleed someone, and from where.

The stars also governed when it was best to sow and pick your herbs. The *Gardener's Labyrinth*, the first popular book on gardening to appear in English, was published in 1577. The author, Thomas Hill, goes into great detail as to the correct astrological time to plant the various types of seeds. Here is some of his advice:

The daily experience is to the Gardener, as a Schoolmaster to instruct him, how much it availeth and hindreth, that seeds to be sown, plants to be set, yea Cions to be grafted (in this or that time) having herein regard, not to the time especially of the year, as the Sunne altereth the same but also the Moons increase and wane, yea to the sign she occupieth, and places both above and under the earth. To the aspects also of the other Planets, whose beams and influence both quicken, comfort, preserve, and maintain or else nip, wither, drie, consume, and destroy by sundry means, the tender seeds, plants, yea and grafts . . .[7]

Running alongside the 'official' medical theories of the day there was also an undercurrent of magic. Here is an example, again taken from Markham's *The English Housewife* under the heading 'For teeth that are loose': 'First let them blood, then take hartshorn or ivory, and red pimpernel, and bruise them well together, then put it into a linen cloth and lay it to the teeth, and it will fasten them.'[8] Hartshorn and ivory would both be associated with teeth, so that to the Tudors it would seem logical that applying hardshorn to teeth would strengthen them.

Another idea was that anything that was especially rare and costly would be a useful cure. The use of 'unicorn's horn' (probably rhinoceros horn) and of 'Bezoar stone' (which is found in certain Asiatic goats) are examples of this, but then the Tudors were hardly alone in this belief. Every age considers strange and expensive substances to be either cure-alls or aphrodisiacs.

Such, then, were the basics of Tudor medicine. Before considering what exactly women were expected to do in the world of medicine, there needs to be an explanation of how the medical world worked at the time.

At the top of the Tudor medical tree, at least in their own estimation, were the university-trained doctors. Before even starting your medical training, it was necessary first to complete your Bachelor of Arts. Even when you got as far as being taught actual medicine, you would find your training very academic, and based purely on the writings of the medical masters of the past, especially those of Galen. This was an age, too, when respect for those in authority was drummed into you from your first years, and that respect was extended to academic authority. Questioning the accuracy of these ancient authorities was seen in the same light as questioning the Bible. As late as 1559 Dr John Geynes was cited before the Congregated College of Physicians for questioning Galen and he was forced to sign a humble recantation before being received back into the College. The case of Dr Geynes shows that these beliefs were being questioned, but such harsh opposition to change slowed the advance of medical thought.[9]

The low standard of English medical training did not help the situation. Most of the better doctors, such as Andrew Boorde, spent time training abroad, especially at the University of Montpellier, although even there medical training was based too much on theory, as the theoretical and practical sides of medicine had become separated over the centuries.

In the thirteenth century Pope Innocent III at the Council of Tours had forbidden those in holy orders to shed blood. The idea was, of course, to stop them fighting battles, but it was taken to mean also that surgery should not be carried out by such people. Surgery therefore became divorced from the academic study of medicine; physicians became more and more absorbed in the study of abstract theory; and surgery was treated as a craft, without any particular academic study attached to it. The fact that physicians also studied many ancient Arab texts made this situation worse, as the Arabs believed that touching a diseased body made you unclean, so that the doctors tended not to examine their patients themselves.

By the late fifteenth century physicians often did not even meet their patients, especially as apothecaries (the Tudor version of modern pharmacists) tended to act as go-between between patient and doctor. The general belief that the imbalance of the humours caused disease also allowed doctors to merely examine their patient's urine, so that the urine flask became the symbol of a doctor's profession, as can be seen from plate 21, showing an Elizabethan doctor as depicted on a painted platter. This obviously laid the physician open to practical jokes, leading to this heartfelt plea from Robert Recorde, in his *Urinall of Physicke* published in 1559: '. . . likewise, I shall enjoin all men not to mock and jest with any physician (as some light-wits do), tempting them with beastes stale instead of man's urine . . . and much other fowle things.'[10]

A doctor's training was so academic that it often did not even include dissecting a human body. Where dissections were carried out, the professor of surgery sat on a high chair reading his lecture whilst a menial known as a 'demonstrator' did the actual dissection.

It was not surprising that medical ideas stagnated in such a climate. However in the sixteenth century new ideas came flooding into medicine, just as they did in other areas. The best example is the attitude to dissection, which gradually became part of medical training, with student doctors actually dissecting bodies themselves so that they could learn firsthand how the body was really made up. Text books such as Vesalius's *De Humani Corporis Fabrica* became available, based upon the author's own experience and observations of dissection.

This did not mean that Tudor medical treatment was vastly different from that of the Middle Ages. The practical effects of the new thinking were not really felt at the time; rather it laid the foundations for the discoveries of the seventeenth century. The main advance was that doctors began to come out of their ivory towers and to take a more practical attitude to medicine. It did not change the fact that university-trained doctors, whether highly respected or not, were very expensive, and well beyond the price of most people.

Ordinary people were more likely to go to the second important body of men in Tudor medicine, the apothecaries. They were supposed to give free advice, and only charge for the remedies they sold as a result. They did not get as far as becoming a separate company in the sixteenth century, but their social status did rise during the period, and they become increasingly reputable.

The barber-surgeons were the third great force in the Tudor medical establishment. They did everything from pulling teeth to the removal of tumours, the setting of broken limbs and the amputations of those limbs too badly damaged to be saved. It was barber-surgeons, rather than doctors, who would accompany armies and sail on ships like the *Mary Rose* to look after the illnesses and injuries of the fighting men. The standard of training for the barber-surgeons seems to have been raised in Tudor times. They were incorporated into a company in London in 1540, and had a portrait painted by Holbein to celebrate the event. Their training was mostly practical, but by the later sixteenth century there were examinations for the apprentices (although how many actually took them is unknown). The London apprentices served seven years, and had to attend a weekly lecture on surgery, and those in other cities such as York, Norwich and Bristol seem to have had a similar education. However, those in Newcastle and Oxford were not so strictly trained, which highlights the constant problem with Tudor medicine.[11] Where you lived determined what help was available to you.

The above list of medical practitioners suggests that there was plenty of skilled medical help available in sixteenth-century England, but unfortunately this was not the case. For one thing, the number of formally-trained practitioners was never high enough to meet the need. This was something that was recognized even in government circles. In 1512 an act had been passed laying down that nobody should practise physic or surgery, except graduates of Oxford or Cambridge, unless licensed by the bishop of his diocese. The fee for unlicensed practice was set at the high price of £5 per month. The preamble to the act gave a list of those to whom the act was aimed, who included 'common artificers, as smiths, weavers, and women that boldly and customarily take upon them great cures and things of great difficulty, in which they partly use sorcery and witchcraft . . . to the . . . grevious hurt, damage and destruction of the king's liege people.' The setting up of the Royal College of Physicians in 1518 also limited those allowed to practise medicine.

In 1542, however, this act was amended, exempting from the penalties 'divers honest persons, as well men as women, whom God hath endowed with the knowledge of the nature kind and operation of certain herbs, roots and waters, and the using and ministering to them to such as be pained with customable disease'. They were only allowed to practise on the understanding that they did so without fee. The licensed doctors did not want these people interfering with their livelihood, but they also recognized that they were unable to meet public demand on their own.

The fact that women are singled out for mention in both acts gives us a clue as to how central the role of women was to Tudor medicine. The housewife was responsible for the comfort and well-being of her family, which naturally included an understanding of how to look after them when they were ill. Markham rather plays down her role, saying that 'we must confess that the depth and secrets of this most excellent art of physic is far beyond the capacity of the most skilful women, as lodging only in the breast of the learned professors . . .'[12]

However, his own book supplies cures for ailments ranging from a headache to the plague, broken bones and coping with serious bleeding, which suggests that women were expected to deal with most medical problems. At this time most people lived in the country where there was highly unlikely to be an apothecary, let alone a barber-surgeon or a doctor. The women just had to be able to cope.

It is very difficult to get an accurate picture of women practising professional medicine at this time. We get glimpses of them at work through letters and literature, and through court records when their work offended the establishment, but that is all. Most information is available concerning their work as midwives, which is discussed in Chapter Two. The lower-class women are the most elusive as even by the sixteenth century many of them were not literate, and their cures and ideas were passed down from mother to daughter by word of mouth. Most of these women only appear in records when on trial for witchcraft.

The local witch or wise woman would have been the only general practitioner available to most people. Many of the cures used by them must have been based on years of trial and error by generations of women, so that it is not surprising that they made some useful discoveries and must often have been more successful than the professional university-trained doctors. Wise women, for example, used ergot for labour pains, and ergot derivatives are still used to hasten labour. They also used belladonna to inhibit uterine contractions when a miscarriage threatened. Belladonna is still used as an anti-spasmodic today.[13] Witches also used charms and other magic, so doubtless not all their cures were successful but their skills were much in demand.

Wise women, despite their popularity with the poor people who were their patients, were despised and even feared by those in authority. Perhaps the fact that they were obviously sometimes more successful than doctors stung professional pride. Paracelsus, the sixteenth-century doctor who pioneered the use of pharmaceutical drugs, was impressed by them and even maintained that he had learnt all he knew from witches, but he was a very controversial figure who even went as far as to burn the works of the accepted medical authorities of the time, Galen and Avicenna, in the public square at Strasbourg. Sadly, most of the information we have about wise women comes from accounts of witch trials.

Witch-hunting took place between the fourteenth and seventeenth centuries and was carried out with varying ferocity in different countries at different times. It was always aimed at the female peasant population and had sinister undercurrents, which mostly had very little to do with whether or not the women were effective doctors. It is interesting that even the persecutors of witches often testify to the success of some of these women. Here is a quote from a leading seventeenth-century English witch-hunter:

For this must always be remembered, as a conclusion, that by witches we understand not only those which kill and torment, but all Diviners, Charmers, Jugglers, all Wizards commonly called wise men and women . . . and in the same number we reckon all Witches which do no hurt but good, which do not spoil and destroy, but save and deliver . . . It were a thousand times better for the land if all Witches, but especially the blessing Witch, might suffer death.[14]

Even a violent opponent of 'witches' had to admit that some of them could 'save and deliver'.

As long as women did not try to become professional healers, their medical skills were valued even by those in authority. *The Paston Letters*, everyday correspondence of the wealthy Paston family covering most of the fifteenth century, make numerous references to medical matters, as the women of the family exchange cures and fuss over the health of the men. One example is a letter written from John Paston III to his wife, Margery:

Mistress Margery

I recommend me to you. And I pray you in all haste possible to send me by the next sure messenger that you can get a large poultice of your flos unguentorum [flower of ointments] for the King's Attorney, James Hobart, for his disease is but an ache in the knee. He is the man who brought you and me together, and I would give £40 that you could with your plaster part him from his pain. But when you send me the poultice, you must send me writing how it should be laid to and taken from his knee, and how long it should abide on his knee without removal, and how long the plaster will last and whether or not he must wrap any more clothes about the plaster to keep it warm. And God be with you.[15]

It is interesting that the Paston women did not have much faith in professional doctors. Margaret Paston made the following pithy observation to her husband, after having seen doctors do little good in other family cases: 'Also for Goddys sake be war what medesyyns ye take of any fysissyans of London: I schal never trust to hem because of your fadir and my onkyl, whoys sowlys God asoyle.'[16] The wealthy lady was still supposed to call in a doctor to deal with really serious cases, but as Margaret's words suggest, many women must have wondered if it was worth the fee.

Fiction is a good reflection of the feelings of any age and in the fiction of the Middle Ages great faith is set in the medical skills of women. In Malory's *Morte Darthur* the King of Ireland happily places Tristan in the care of his daughter, La Belle Iseult, 'because she was a noble surgion.' King Mark also sends for 'alle maner of leches and surgeons bothe unto men and wymmen . . .'. In the earlier Middle Ages, Nicolette, a Saracen slave, puts her lover's dislocated shoulder back in place after he falls from his horse whilst distracted with thoughts of love for her.[17]

Having established that women were expected to be skilled in medicine, what sort of training and knowledge would a woman have? It is difficult to know as not many women wrote down either their thoughts or knowledge about medicine or what they knew. In the sixteenth century we begin to get more of an idea with the publication of books on housewifery but it is difficult to know to what extent these books give the full picture. The books are aimed mostly at the middle-class market, and make assumptions such as the ability to afford some of the more expensive ingredients from the apothecary, and the possession of the still room and all the equipment that was needed. The arts and cures of wise women, for example, are difficult to pin down. Women were, of course, excluded from universities and so from the forefront of medicine but the bulk of the work of caring for the sick still fell to them.

The most obvious job that fell to them was nursing. At this time the vast majority of people would have been cared for at home even when seriously ill. Hospitals did exist, but they were not always designed for the care of the sick – Christ's Hospital in London was set up for the care of orphans, for example. Even those hospitals which did care for the sick usually cared for the very poor who simply had no-one to look after them. St Bartholomew's and St Thomas's Hospitals in London both looked after sick, aged or otherwise infirm beggars at this time, but even so most nursing was done at home. In the parish of Aldgate in London in the late sixteenth century many poor people found sick on the street were carried not to one of the hospitals but to local people's houses. Their stories are still to be found in the parish registers. Here is the story of Peter Nicholson who died on 19 December 1594:

> Peter Nycholson a singleman or batcheler and as was sayd he was a sayler being borne at Barking in Essex who being verie sicke in the striete before the signe of the harshorne a brewhouse was caried by the head borowe [one of the parish officers] to the house of William Landie a lyghterman dwelling in morlyes rentte . . . where he dyed.[18]

The sheer amount of work involved in nursing a seriously ill person, who would today be taken to hospital to be cared for by specialist nurses, must have been enormous, especially when all the normal burdens of keeping house were added to it. People today, with all the benefits of modern medicine, not only generally recover much faster than their sixteenth-century ancestors, but are ill much less often. A far greater percentage of women's time must have been taken up with nursing her family than we would expect today.

Most women would have learnt their medicine from their mothers, but the development of printing meant that, for middle and upper class women at least, they could add to their knowledge by reading. Medical books written in English began to appear, aimed at the general reader, but not without objection from the medical establishment. Real 'academic' books were still written in Latin and even Sir Thomas Elyot, a rich and well-connected courtier, had to include a defence for writing his *Castel of Helth* in English in the preface of its second edition. Such books, however, remained firmly based on the principles of the four humours so women were better served by the increasing range of herbals which were slowly becoming available.

Today we imagine herbals to be books of botanical illustrations of herbs with a description of the herb and a discussion of its various uses. This was something that was only just beginning to evolve in the sixteenth century. *Banckes Herbal*, the first book printed in England to deal only with herbs and published in 1525, was not even illustrated. The *Grete Herball* or *Arbolayre translated out of ye Frensshe into Englysshe*, one of the most influential herbals to be published in England in the sixteenth century, had illustrations, but these were so vague that they did little to help identify the plants. A wonderful example of this is that the same illustration was used to identify the cherry as the deadly nightshade! Fortunately, the figure looks little like either plant so probably there were no very serious results.[19]

The most famous herbal of the time is Gerard's *Herbal*, published in 1597. Despite its influence, it was not quite all it seemed. It is really a herbal written by a doctor named Dodeous early in the century, and largely translated by a Dr Prest who died before his work was completed. Gerard, himself a barber-surgeon, took the work over but really took over more than he could cope with. Norton, the publisher who produced the work, rented around 1,800 woodcuts to illustrate the volume and poor Gerard found he could not even match many of them to the text, although, of course, he didn't admit this in print; and from the magnificent coloured frontispiece in the Bodleian Library's edition he seems quite the master of his subject. Fortunately his work was later edited by a London apothecary called Thomas Johnson, and the 'Johnson Gerard', first published in 1633, was not only full of new entries, so that it was half as long again as the original version, but was also much more accurate. Even so, the full volume cost forty two shillings and sixpence unbound or forty eight shillings bound. At that price it would have been well out of the reach of most women.[20]

Having correctly identified her herbs, the housewife's job was far from over. Fresh herbs were only available in season, and so they had to be preserved in some way

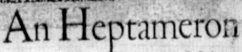

An Heptameron

of Ciuill Discourses.

Containing: The Christmasse Exercise of sundrie well Courted Gen-
demen and Gentlewomen.

In whose behauiours, the better
sort, may see a represêtation of their own Vertues:
And the Inferiour, may learne such Rules of Ciuil Go-
uernmêt, as wil rase out the Blemish of their basenesse:

Wherin, is Renowned, the Vertues, of a most Honou-
rable and braue mynded Gentleman.

And herein, also, (as it were in a Mirrour) the Vnmaried
may see the Defectes whiche Eclipse the Glorie of MARIAGE:
And the wel Maried, as in a Table of Houshôlde Lawes, may cull
out needefull Preceptes to establysh their good Fortune.

A Worke, intercoursed with Ciuyll Pleasure, to reaue
tediousnesse from the Reader: and garnished with Morall Noates
to make it profitable, to the Regarder.

The Reporte, of George Whetstone. Gent.

Formæ, nulla fides.

AT LONDON,

Printed by Richard Iones,

at the Signe of the Rose and the Crowne,
neare Holburne Bridge. 3. Feb. 1582.

rontispiece of *An Heptameron of Civil Discourses* by Richard Jones, one of the
any marriage guidance books produced in the sixteenth century. *(British Library)*

Two sixteenth-century wedding rings. The inscription inside the open one reads in Latin, 'That which God has joined let no man divide'. *(British Museum)*

Sir Henry Unton's wedding, with a masque being performed in the foreground.
(National Portrait Gallery, London)

lutus est, secundinam inquam, cum duabus reliquis tunicis, de qui-
bus supra dictum est, perrumpat,
& pro huius figuræ ratione se ad
partum expediat.

Hac indicatione obstetrices &
aliæ quæ interdum prægnantibus
adsunt mulieres, veros partus do-
lores obseruent: qui re ipsa nihil
aliud quàm perfecti iam infan-
tis impetus sunt, quibus impellun-
tur & rotantur, deorsumque ad
inferiora exeundi gratia conten-
dunt. Ruptis enim ex impetu mē-
branis & reclusa matrice, humo-
res diffluere incipiunt, quibus li-
beratus iam infans mox aerem
sentit, & huius vitæ cupidus, exi-
tum matricis versus voluitur, ca-
pite orificio matricis obuerso. Et
hæc legitimi & maxime naturalis
partus forma est, si caput primum
ad exitum ducatur, deductis ad
latera manibus & super coxas ap-
plicatis, vti præsens adiecta figura
ostendit. Non naturalis autem
partus dicitur, si harum conditio-
num aliqua defuerit. Curabit itaq;
obstetrix, vt maturè ad quemuis
partum excipiendum, apto sedili,
cultro, spongia, vinculis, calidoque
ex lilijs oleo, quo & parturientis
vterū & manus suas cōmode per-
ungat, instructa sit.

Partus dolo-
res quid.

Naturalis pa-
tus qui.

E 3 CA-

Two of the diagrams from Reuff's *De conceptu et generatione hominis,*
published in 1580. *(British Museum)*

Mailolica plate which would originally have formed part of a set of china to be used during a lady's confinement. *(Fitzwilliam Museum, Cambridge)*

De mixtura vtriufque fexus feminis, eiufque fubftantia & forma.

P *Oftquam autem vterus, quod genitale fœminei fexus membrum*
eft, virigenituram conceperit, fuum quoque femen illi admifcet,

𝄢 3   *ita*

The influence of the stars was thought to be vital. Here a baby's horoscope is cast as soon as it is born. Scene from Jacob Reuff's *De conceptu et generatione hominis*, published 1580. *(British Museum)*

DE CONCEPTV

ET GENERATIONE

HOMINIS: DE MATRICE ET EIVS

PARTIBVS, NEC NON DE CONDITIONE IN-

FANTIS IN VTERO, ET GRAVIDARVM CVRA ET OFFICIO:
De partu & parturientium infantiumq́; cura omnifaria: De differentijs non
naturalis partus & earundem curis: De Mola alijsq́; falsis vteri tumoribus,
simulq́ue de abortibus & monstris diuersis, nec non de conceptus signis varijs: De sterilitatis causis diuersis, & de præcipuis Matricis ægritudini-
bus, omniumq́ue horum curis varijs, libri sex, opera claris-
simi viri IACOBI RVEFFI, Chirurgi Tigu-
rini, quondam congesti.

Nunc denuò recogniti & in plerisq́ locis castigati, picturis insuper conuenientißimis fœ-
tus primùm in vtero siti, deinde in partu, mox etiam matricis & instrumentorum
ad partum promouendum, & extrahendum pertinentium, illustrati, ornati, & in
vsum eorum qui parturientibus, & obstetricibus consulere debent, typis euulgati.

Francoforti ad Mœnum. Anno M. D. LXXX.

The delivery over, the baby is washed and the mother receives congratulations.
From Jacob Reuff *De conceptu et generatione hominis*, published 1580.
(British Museum)

A woman and children,
sketched by Holbein in

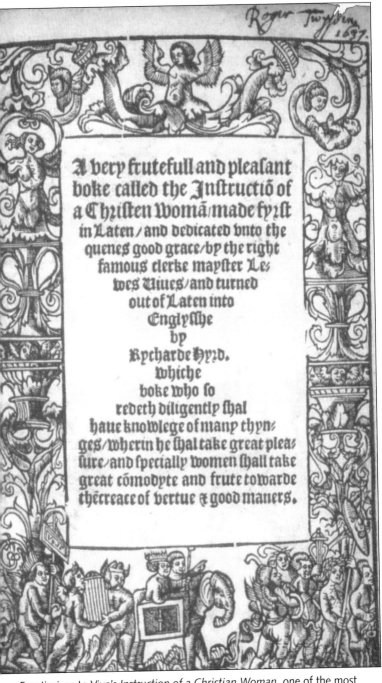

A very frutefull and pleasant
boke called the Instructió of
a Christen Womã/made fyrst
in Laten/and dedicated vnto the
quenes good grace/by the right
famous clerke mayster Le=
wes Uiues/and turned
out of Laten into
Englysshe
by
Rycharde Hyrd.
whiche
boke who so
redeth diligently shal
haue knowlege of many thyn=
ges/wherin he shal take great plea=
sure/and specially women shall take
great cõmodyte and frute towarde
thẽcreace of vertue & good maners.

Frontispiece to Vive's *Instruction of a Christian Woman*, one of the most
influential books of the sixteenth century. *(British Library (G11884))*

A mother and daughter. The little girl is dressed as an adult and would be expected to behave as one too.
(Lacock Abbey, The National Trust (Courtauld Institute of Art))

Title page from *The Needles Excellency* published in 1640 showing a virtuous lady hard at work with her needle. Young girls were brought up never to be idle. (British Library (C31h30TP))

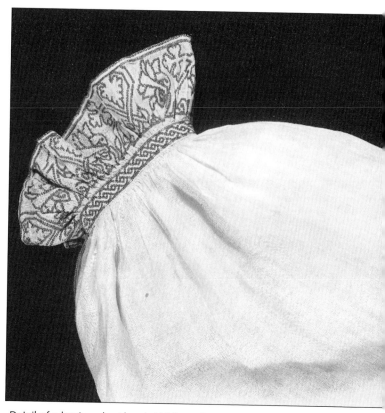

Detail of a boy's embroidered shirt from the sixteenth century. An example of the type of embroidery a better-off girl would learn.
(Victoria and Albert Museum)

In the days when proper drainage pipes were a luxury, waste water would be poured into a 'sink' like this one, from where it could drain easily back into the earth without making the surface soil muddy. (*from Dorothy Hartley* Water in England, *Macdonald, London, 1964*)

An example of Tudor underwear. This is a boy's shirt from the period. The lady's shift was very similar, but longer. (*Victoria and Albert Museum*)

A sixteenth-century washerwoman at work – washing was always considered to be a woman's work. *(Julie Anne Hudson)*

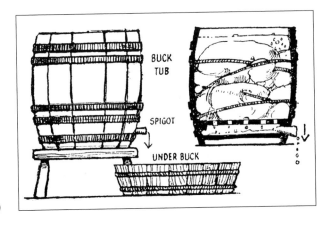

...ow to 'ley ...e buck'. The ...en had to ...e folded and ...aced in the ...ucking tub in ...certain way ...ensure that ...e ley flowed ...eely around ...and then ...ained away. *...rom Dorothy ...artley* Water ...England, *...acdonald, ...ondon, 1964)*

BUCK TUB

SPIGOT

UNDER BUCK

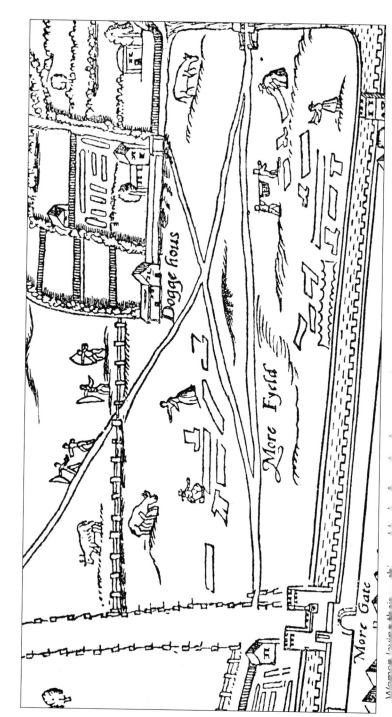

Dogge hous

More Fyeld

More Gate

Women laying out their clothes

The grete herball

whiche geueth parfyt knowlege and vnd

ndyng of all maner of herbes & there gracyous vertues whiche god ha
deyued for our prosperous welfare and heith/for they hele & cure all man
dyseases and sekenesses that fall or mysfortune to all maner of creatou
god created/practysed by many expert and wyse maysters/as Auicenn
ier. &c. Also it geueth full parfyte vnderstandynge of the booke lately p
by me(Peter treueris)named the noble experiens of the vertuous ha
arke of surgery.

Heavier clothing fabrics which could not be cleaned effectively needed to be rfumed. Here blooms are being collected to make perfume, and also for use in the kitchen. *(British Library (C27L1))*

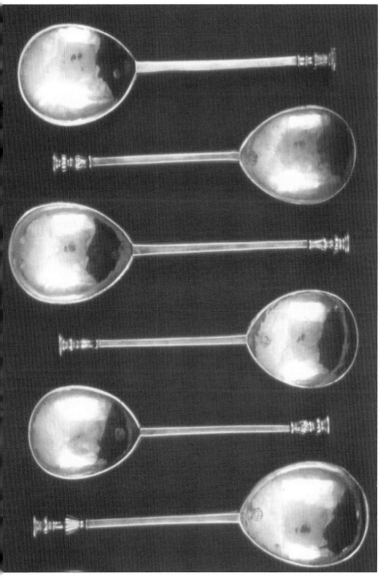

ilver spoons, now in the British Museum. It was usual to bring your own spoon
to the table. *(British Museum)*

Butirum is butter. In the fy

gre it is hote / and colde in th

de. The best butter is it is

A woman churns butter. Dairying was hard work, but it was the tradition that t
profits of the dairy belonged to the woman of the house. *(British Library (sig k*
C27L1 cic))

An Elizabethan plate showing a doctor holding a urine flask. The inscription reads, ' . . . The earthe my faults doth hide, The World my cares doe see, What youthe and Time effectes, Is oft scribed on mee . . .' *(The Bodleian Library/ University of Oxford)*

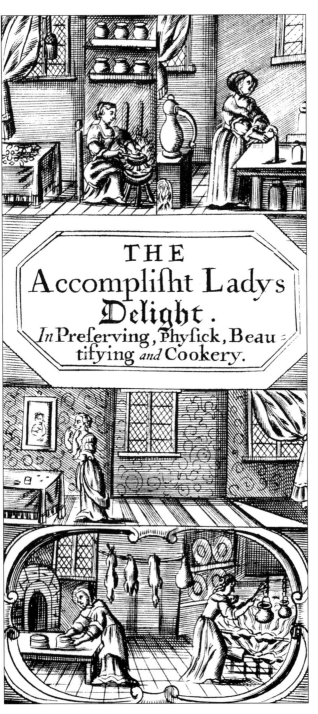

THE
Accomplisht Ladys
Delight.
In Preserving, Physick, Beau=
tifying *and* Cookery.

Title page from *The Accomplis Lady's Del in Preserv Physick, Beautifyin and Cooke* The top tw ladies can seen at wo in a still ro *(British Lit (Douce p. 412))*

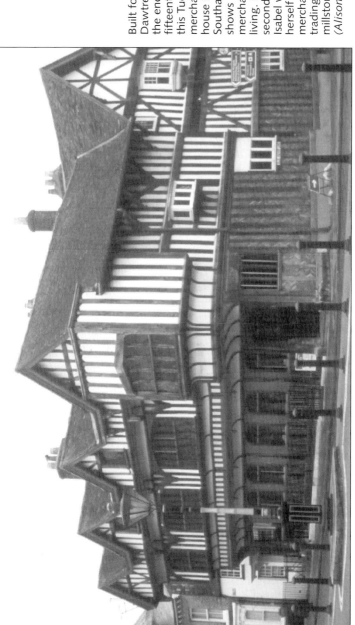

Built for Sir John Dawtrey at the end of the fifteenth century, this Tudor merchant's house in Southampton shows how well merchants were living. Dawtrey's second wife Isabel was herself a merchant, trading in millstones. (*Alison Sim*)

¶A deuout treatise vpon the Pater no=
ster / made fyrst in latyn by the moost fa=
mous doctour mayster Erasmus
Roterodamus / and tourned
in to englisshe by a yong
vertuous and well
lerned gentylwoman of .xix.
yere of age.

Title page of Margaret More Roper's translation of Erasmus's *Devout Treatise Upon the Pater Noster*. (Julie Anne Hudson)

Nicolas Belenian, with certaine of y counsyell sittyng in smithfield.*

The execution of Anne Askew, fom Fox's *Acts and Monuments.* *(British Library)*

An ordinary woman from the *Grete Herbal*. Sadly we have little record of wha[t] such women felt about their lives. *(British Library)*

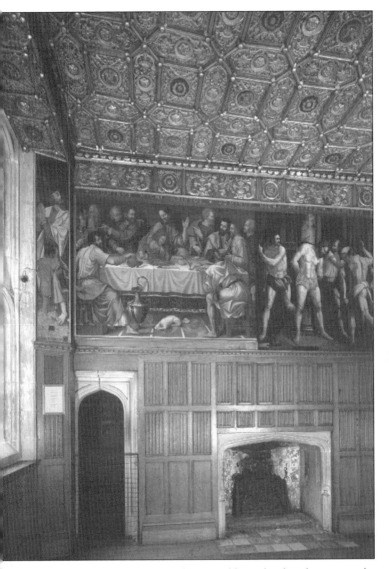

The 'Wolsey Closet', Hampton Court Palace. Wealthy Tudors loved to surround themselves with rich decoration. *(Historic Royal Palaces, Crown Copyright)*

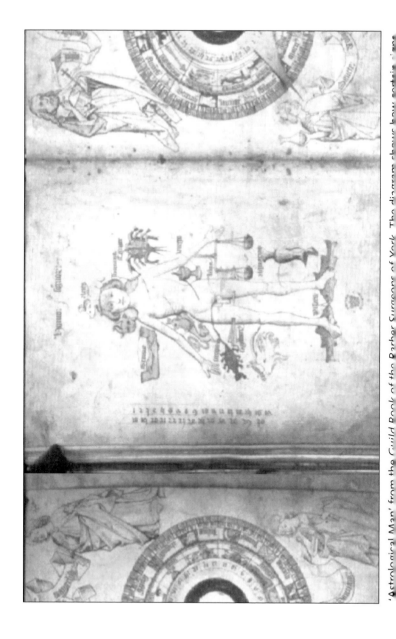

'Astrological Man' from the *Guild Book of the Barber Surgeons of York*. The diagram shows how certain signs

A recreation of a house interior, c. 1600 in the Geffrye Museum, London. This is a well-to-do household, but there are no carpets. Carpets were valuable works of art at the time, not items for walking on. (*Trustees of the Geffrye Museum*)

Hardwick Hall, one of the houses built by Bess of Hardwick.
(National Trust Photographic Library)

Elizabeth I saw that all religious precious objects which she did not approve of
were destroyed. The Stonyhouse Salt, now in the British Museum, was made from
jewels taken from churches. *(British Museum)*

One of the garden pavilions at Montacute House, an example of the type of construction often used for banquets. *(National Trust*

for use over the rest of the year. The housewife also had to make up salves, syrups, candies (which were used in medicine and not only as sweets) and sweet waters for use as medicines. The latter in particular were a great fashion in the sixteenth century. These were distilled waters and every lady who could have afforded one would have had a still room.

The idea of distilling was to preserve the essence of various herbs all year round. Distilled waters were also a very convenient form of medicine, being easily added to anything from salves to candies. The still room would be used generally for the production of medicines but the great pride of the Tudor lady, judging from the housewifery books of the time, was her still. There are often separate sections on distilling in the books. Sir Hugh Plat's *Delightes for Ladies* includes twenty-five such recipes in his 'Secrets in Distillation' section, and Gervase Markham, thirty-eight.

The uses of the recipes are not all medicinal; Sir Hugh, for example, provides a recipe for 'A Scottish Handwater'[21] designed to be added to ordinary water to make 'a very sweet washing water'. There are also some waters, such as rosewater, which are used both medicinally and for everything from cosmetics to cooking. Ladies seem to have used so much rosewater that Sir Hugh even provides a way of preserving roses in order 'to distill rosewater at Michaelmas and to have a good yeeld as at any other time of the yeare'. Ladies were making so much rosewater that they were buying the roses in and obviously they were cheapest, '7. pence or 8. pence the bushell' according to Sir Hugh, when the roses were in season.[22]

Sixteenth-century women, though not allowed to be at the forefront of Tudor medicine, were certainly the backbone of the science. Certainly many a man must have agreed with Chaucer's sentiments as quoted from the 'Merchant's Tale':

> Wel may the sike man biwaille and wepe
> Ther as ther nys no wyf the house to kepe.

SEVEN

WOMEN AND BUSINESS LIFE

To the modern world it seems odd that Tudor women played such an active part in business life, given that they were expected to be humble and submissive and to centre their attention on their homes and families. In the sixteenth century work still revolved very much around the home, so that the split between work and family life was nowhere near as obvious as it is to us, and was sometimes non-existent. A woman might brew beer for use at home, but sell the surplus, just as her dairy might provide produce for both the home and the market-place. A wealthy merchant's wife, who would expect to look after the family accounts, might well also do the accounts for her husband's business. A few intrepid women even ran businesses in their own right and handled a great deal of money. A woman with a good head for business was certainly an asset to her family. There were also quite significant numbers of women who never married and therefore had no choice but to earn an independent living.

At the top of society there were some wealthy women who handled quite large amounts of trade. The most famous of these were the fifteenth-century silk women. In England the silk women did not weave silk cloth, but dealt in raw silk thread, and in the processes that went into making it up into a variety of products such as ribbons, laces and girdles. Silk laces were not what we would think of today as lace, but twisted silk cords which had a whole variety of uses from attaching seals to documents to decorating and holding together rich people's clothing. They were also made into a variety of finished articles such as cauls for grand ladies to wear over their hair. The silk women also dealt in the finished goods.

In continental Europe, for example in Paris, the silk women even had their own special gild.[1] In England, though there was no formal guild, the silk women were still a respected body. They were strongest in London, where the market for the luxury goods they sold was greatest, but they also existed in other towns. In 1482 the preamble of a petition they sent to the king talks of 'the hole craft of Silkewerk of the Cite of London and all other Cities, Townes, Boroghes and Vilages of this Realme of England'.[2]

The silk women took apprentices, just as men did in other crafts, and the apprentices served under the same sort of terms as boy apprentices did. Two indentures survive in the Public Records Office,[3] one for a Yorkshire girl and another for a girl from Lincolnshire, both of whom were bound apprentices in London. The indentures bind the girls to both the silk woman and her husband, but state that the girls are to learn the woman's craft. The girls are to serve for seven years, to behave well, are not to waste their master and mistress's goods and are to cherish their business. In return, the master and mistress promise to take charge of and instruct their apprentice in the wife's craft, to chastise her in meet fashion and to give her food, clothing, footwear, a bed and all other necessities.

The master and mistress of an apprentice were not just employers, but very much took the place of the child's parents, and took responsibility for its behaviour both during and outside working hours. As the parents could well have lived miles away there was really no option. As a result, the apprentice–master relationship was often fraught with difficulties as business and emotional matters became mixed up together.

Apprentices were not only taught a craft, but were also given training in how to run a business, with a view to them setting up on their own later on. Apprentices became very involved with their mistress's businesses and even bought and sold goods on their mistress's behalf. To make matters more confusing, apprentices were often allowed to do some trading on their own account. It was not surprising that disputes developed, and the silk women were no exception to this. An account of such a disagreement, between Joan Woulbarowe and her former mistress, survives. The two women got into dispute over what exactly had happened to some silk that Joan delivered for her mistress, and there were also claims that Joan had bought silk for herself rather than her mistress.[4] The dispute evidently became quite bitter, with both women doubtless feeling that they had been taken advantage of by the other.

Managing the apprentices was only one of the problems the silk women faced. Some of them become involved in complicated large-scale transactions which many men must have envied. The raw silk thread was not produced here in England, but was bought from Italian merchants. Jane Langton, the widow of a saddler, became bound for payment for silk goods worth £300 15s to two Genoa merchants in the place of her daughter-in-law Agnes who died whilst away at Stourbridge fair. There is nothing to show whether Agnes was simply a middleman, or whether she was buying the silk for further working, but certainly the family were heavily involved in the silk business. Jane Langton herself is described as a silk woman in her will dated 1475, and Elizabeth, her son's second wife, is likely to have been the silk woman who supplied £101 17s worth of goods to the royal family in 1503.[5]

The position of women in other prestigious trades is not quite so clear. Certainly they were not involved in the government of any of the guilds, which severely restricted their influence. Guilds were trade organizations which not only regulated working conditions, terms of apprenticeship and so forth, but also provided charitable support for members and their families who had fallen on hard times. The guilds were also very important social groups, and met several times a year for feasts. The most powerful London guilds, like the Fishmongers and the Goldsmiths, also played a large role in the running of the city so that guild membership was an important privilege.

Only five out of the five hundred guilds in England excluded women and references to apprentices suggest that girls as well as boys served their time in various trades. A statute of 1406, for example, states that no man or woman worth under 20 shillings a year could apprentice his son or daughter to any craft within any city or borough.[6] The mention of daughters was not just academic. In 1423, for example, Agnes Snell of Hoo, Kent, was bound apprentice to Agnes Haunsarde for ten years.[7] However, by the sixteenth century there were very few girls apprenticed to the skilled and prestigious trades. Women who became guild members usually did so through marriage. If their husband died and they remarried, the new husband could also become a full guild member. This was a very useful asset but the woman still only belonged to the guild because of her husband's trade rather than due to any skills of her own. If her new husband was of another trade to the previous husband the woman had to leave the guild.

It is sometimes difficult to tell exactly what women's involvement in the guilds was. They were certainly involved in the social life, and, considering that knowing the right people was even more important in the sixteenth century than it is today, this was no small matter. The Drapers, for example, had a hall for the ladies' use where they sometimes held dinners separately from the men, although they usually dined in the hall with their husbands.[8] No doubt some women used these occasions to talk business with the right people and to further their husbands' businesses if they got the opportunity, but equally others must just have enjoyed these events as social occasions.

The guilds also find themselves remembered in rich widows' wills. Joyce Williamson left £100 to the Clothworkers' Company in the late sixteenth century, suggesting that she must have been an active member. Joyce also had an apprentice, her goddaughter, to whom she left £1,000, so she obviously had a personal business involvement with the company too.[9] A woman's involvement in a guild must have depended very much on her personality and on her relationship with her husband.

Extending guild membership to women through their husbands was generally far more than a social courtesy. Widows were permitted to carry on their husbands' businesses after his death, and even to take over the training of apprentices. Some took over just for a short period, of about a year or so, in order to wind the business up, but others carried on for several years. Out of the seventy widows who were left print shops in the period 1553–1640 as many as fifty got rid of the shops within four years, but others carried on their businesses for much longer. Widows represented a tenth of all publishers in the period.[10] The widows of nearly a third of aldermen of the City of London carried on some kind of trading after their husbands' death.[11]

Some widows were obviously very efficient businesswomen and carried on large-scale trade for some years. Dionisia Holme of Beverley in Yorkshire continued large-scale export of wool and wool fells (sheepskins with the wool still attached) between her husband's death in 1471 and her own in 1485. In their letters the Johnsons mention a variety of widows who had large-scale businesses. Jane Rawe is one such woman, who ran a private exchange business, travelling between Hazebrouck, London, Antwerp and Calais as the need arose. Another is Mrs Baynham who traded in wool, wine and herrings, besides running a boarding house in Calais for her stapler friends and also running hundreds of acres of farmland.[12]

Most widows were not as fortunate as these wealthy and privileged women. The circumstances in London were by no means typical of the country as a whole, London being so much larger and wealthier than the other cities of England at the time. The merchants of the Staple in Calais, like the Johnsons, were also too wealthy a section of the population to be considered typical. A study of the conditions for widows in the rather smaller town of Salisbury gives an idea of what it was like to live in provincial England at the time.[13]

Salisbury had been very wealthy in the fifteenth century, but in the sixteenth century it went into a decline. Evidence from Salisbury shows how very difficult it seems to have been for less wealthy widows to maintain their husbands' businesses. To keep the business going a widow would need tools, a workshop, a labour force and experience of running a business herself. In the parish of St Thomas, one of the wealthier areas, about half of the widows had moved away from the marital home (and therefore away from the workshop too) in under a year after the spouse's death. Many more had moved away, often to remarry, after only a year of independence. Of course not all of these women's husbands had their own businesses, so this is a rather rough statistic, but even in cases where the women remained in the old marital home a male relative often took charge of the shop. Only a minority of widows, it seems, would have had their husband's workshop at their disposal.

It is harder to trace what happened to a man's stock and equipment after he died. There is often no mention at all of these items in wills. Some men did leave their tools for their wife's use, such as Nicholas Atkinson who, although he left all the tools of his trade as professional embroiderer to his son, nevertheless added, 'I will my wife shall keepe and use [the tools] as long as she doth use my trade.'[14] Tools were also sometimes left to children or apprentices. Clearly the widow could not expect them as a matter of course.

Some women did have the workforce they needed to keep a business going. Taking the information for the years 1585, 1593 and 1594, about 9 per cent of households which were run by a woman rather than a man had apprentices. Some women even had several apprentices. In 1625 a census was taken to allow the authorities to find out how many paupers there were in the now rather impoverished town. The poor children were to be taught a trade, and details of the people to whom they were apprenticed survive. The names include a number of women who only had one apprentice each, and so presumably were only in business in a small way. However, some ran larger concerns. The wife of Launcelot Russel took no fewer than six children and Alice Swift had not only six apprentices working for her, but also three servants.[15]

Business experience is obviously difficult to judge, as it is not the kind of thing that was recorded, but certainly it was not lacking in some women. The list of free citizens for Salisbury in 1612 includes women trading alone as well as merchants, tanners, butchers, pewterers and people running inns. The Salisbury Corporation Archives also have evidence of women tailors, glovers and maltsters in other records.[16] Even in a provincial town there were, then, women who managed their own businesses of various kinds, although continuing your husband's business after his death was by no means automatic. The women who were able to do this were, as in London, from the more prosperous end of society. What of the women at the other end of the scale?

The only apprenticeship most girls could expect was that of learning 'huswyfrye' as a domestic servant. Sometimes this was done through a formal apprenticeship, sometimes not, but often the girls were also taught some kind of craft. One girl was apprenticed in January 1612 to Elizabeth Deacon, wife of a tailor, to learn both this craft and 'flaxdressing' whilst two months later Mary Gunter was apprenticed to learn both domestic skills and knitting.[17] These extra skills could be well worth learning. The 1570 census of the poor in Norwich includes an entry for a fourteen-year-old girl who was providing the 'chief living' for her father's family by knitting great hose.[18]

Certainly the most common job for young unmarried girls was that of domestic servant. In Ealing in Middlesex in 1599 58 per cent of girls aged 20 to 24 were in service.[19] Despite this fact it was far more prestigious to employ men than women at the time, and grand households, like the royal household, employed men rather than women in this capacity. A few women were employed to do the washing, and the woman of the house might well have a female attendant, but that was all. In Henry VIII's household, apart from the washerwoman, there was only one woman working as a domestic servant, and she was a confectioner. Unfortunately we do not even know her name, nor how she came to be offered the job in the first place.

Less magnificent households had always employed maidservants, and by the end of the sixteenth century when inflation was eating into the incomes of even the well-off, the grander households began to employ more women too. Certainly the wealthy Grace Sherrington employed maidservants[20] at the end of the sixteenth century.

Domestic service was not necessarily an unpleasant option. The girls would be fed, housed and clothed by their employers and for many of them their years in service would be the most prosperous of their lives. There was also a great deal of opportunity to move around different employers if the present situation did not suit them. In Salisbury in the later sixteenth century over half of the domestic servants stayed in their jobs for over a year, but very few for over four years. Most stayed for between one and two years. However, even if a girl worked for good employers and was well fed and clothed, she was still hardly trained with a view to becoming an independent worker, in the way apprentices were in the craft guilds.

Not all domestic servants lived in their master's house. There were several examples of 'charmaids' who came in daily. The authorities generally disliked servants being employed in this way, as they felt that they might easily become unemployed and so be a burden on the parish. This didn't stop the employment of charmaids, or of the washerwomen that so many households relied on. Like so much other women's work, it was unfortunately neither prestigious nor well paid.

A study of other industries suggests that the pattern of giving women the less well-paid work was repeated all too often. The wool trade, in both raw wool and finished cloth, was second in importance only to agriculture in the sixteenth century. Spinning was considered women's work to the extent that 'spinster' still means single woman even today. At the time it was as much a trade for married women as for single. Many families fitted their textile work around running their own smallholding, and many women were spinning more for home use than for sale. They would only sell their work when the rates of pay were highest, just as husbandmen only worked for farmers at harvest time, when wages were best. The work was best paid if women bought their own wool and then sold the thread on, but poorer women who could not afford to do this worked on piece rates, spinning wool provided for them by the middleman and being paid by the pound of wool spun. In Edward VI's time in Norwich the spinsters were having trouble buying wool wholesale as the middlemen were buying it all up.[21]

In the Middle Ages women also wove cloth alongside the men, but in the late fifteenth and early sixteenth centuries, when trade was bad, there were a number of attempts to force them out of the commercial trade. The Norwich weavers, for example, excluded women in 1511 saying 'thei bee not of sufficient powre to werke the said worsteddes as thei owte to be wrought.'[22] As the women had no say in the government of the guilds they had no way of defending themselves against such legislation.

The woollen industry was so important that there was even some attempt to set up a factory system for weaving woollen cloth. John Leland in his *Itinerary*, written between 1535 and 1543, describes the workshop of a weaver which was set up in a church at Malmesbury. Several looms had been moved into the church, but it was still not on the scale of John Winchcombe's household which is described as having two hundred looms in it, with two hundred men weaving, a hundred women carding and two hundred 'maidens' working at other processes.[23] These experiments were not continued as it was felt that having workers assembled in large numbers encouraged them to disobey their master. The government also felt that it made wage-earners too dependent on the clothier, and therefore rather insecure financially. At this time the authorities generally preferred workers to have some sort of smallholding of their own, and not to become over-dependent on one master. After all, if a large-scale employer went bankrupt large numbers of people could then find themselves looking to the parish for support. The factory experiment might also have failed for economic reasons. The clothiers found that they could pay lower wages to the women working at home.

Another source of employment for women was the retail trade. At the higher end of society, rich merchants' wives might well work in their husbands' shops, and even lower down the scale a woman might keep a small shop and might even have served an apprenticeship as a shopkeeper. Far more women were employed in the lower end of the retail trade, as pedlars, who sold haberdashery and other bits and pieces, or regraters, who dealt in perishable goods. In the sixteenth century many people were happy to pay a little more for goods if they were brought to the door, although it was certainly a hard way to earn a living.

Single women, and the poorer widows who did not remarry, found making ends meet particularly hard. The economic odds were certainly stacked against lone women. If a man had a low opinion of his wife, even after his death he could make life difficult for her by virtually excluding her from his will. Thomas Field, a cordwainer of the parish of St Brides, Fleet Street in London did just this. The executorship of his will and the residue of his goods went to three men friends 'in hope and truste yt they will kepe, maintaine, find and relive Constance Field my widow with all things necesssary for this life so far as the goods extend during her natural life.' After Constance's death goods were willed to go to his daughter-in-law, and the apprentice was also relieved of the remainder of his apprenticeship. Even Constance's feather bed was left to a servant.[24]

This was unusual. As the section on marriage shows, most marriage settlements were carefully negotiated so as to ensure that a widow would be left well provided for, and in any case, most men seem to have a better opinion of their wives than Thomas Field had. It was far more likely that a woman would be appointed at least one of the executors of her husband's will, and to be left at least the goods she had brought to the marriage as her dowry. Many men were happy to acknowledge their wife's contribution to the family income. The will of Robert Sydall, clothier of Holbech in Yorkshire, is far more typical, leaving 'to Elizabeth my wife, such vessels and furniture as belongeth to her brewinge and all that stock of money which she hath eyotten by her bakinge and brewinge'.[25] Even so, a woman very much relied on the good will of her husband in this respect. A woman in Constance Field's position was virtually powerless, however unfair the will.

The legal position of women could also hamper their business affairs unless they had their husband's support. Under the law husband and wife were one person. This did not mean that both had equal rights, but that the wife was seen legally as being an extension of her husband. She could not make contracts or even buy goods without her husband's prior consent. A wife could act as her husband's agent and make contracts provided these were previously authorized by him and approved by him afterwards. A woman was a minor under the law, unable to take full responsibility for her actions.[26] A sixteenth-century commentator put it this way:

A married woman cannot make a contract to her husband's loss or prejudice but can if it is to his profit. Thus I can give a married woman a gift and the husband agree to it, but if a married woman make a contract to buy something in the market, this is not valid since the cost may be a burden to her husband. But my wife can buy something for her own use and I can ratify the purchase. If I order my wife to buy necessities and she buys them, I shall be held responsible because of the general authorisation given to her. But if my wife buys things for my household like bread etc without my knowledge, I shall not be held responsible for it even if it was consumed in my household.[27]

As a result, it was impossible for a married woman to get involved in business without her husband's support. There was a way out, at least in towns, for a man who was happy to see his wife have a business, but who did not wish to become involved with any debts she might incur. This was to have the woman declared a 'femme sole', or single woman, at least as far as her business was concerned. This allowed her to plead as if she were a single woman, should her affairs ever bring her in contact with the law; so her husband's goods could not be touched to pay for any debts she incurred.

Women were not above using this legal tangle to their own advantage. On several occasions the silk women's creditors were not able to maintain court actions for debt against them because they had thought that the women were trading as 'femme sole', responsible for their own debts. The women were later discovered to have never been officially registered as 'femme sole' and so were able to escape responsibility for the debts when the creditors began to demand repayment.[28]

A woman who never married would find it impossible to set up any large-scale business because she would have no capital to do it with. Any heiress would find herself married off by her parents or guardians. The women who were left single and had to make their own way in the world had neither the money nor the connections to do very much more than make a living.

There is room for a great deal of study in the area of sixteenth-century women's work, but it does seem that the majority of women were employed in lower-paid work than their male counterparts. As the sixteenth century progressed, opportunities for women in any case decreased, for rich and poor alike. The exact reason for this is not clear, but certainly the position of women in society generally was changing. By the middle of the seventeenth century women were actually formally excluded from many areas, even those in which women had proved themselves competent. The stationers, for example, excluded women in 1640. By the end of the seventeenth century it was considered unusual for a woman to have a thorough knowledge of her husband's business. Pepys had a conversation with a very well-informed merchant's wife and was so surprised by her understanding of business that he records their meeting in his diary.

Another example of this decline is the brewing industry, which had been dominated by women in the Middle Ages, to the extent that the female form of brewer, 'brewster', was used as a blanket term. These women would brew in their own homes. By the early seventeenth century it had become a large-scale business carried out in purpose-built breweries and was dominated by men.[29]

Women in the sixteenth century were still brought up to have an understanding of business, accounts and so on, and even to play a large part in running the family estates, as the chapter on education demonstrates. They were certainly not excluded from business affairs, and many did have an opportunity to show just have capable they could be in this area. However, women's efforts were very much part of their contribution to the family economy and were often a by-product of housekeeping in any case – such as when they sold excess beer, cheese or eggs. They used their skills either to help their husbands' businesses, or to maintain the family interests if they were left alone as widows. Single women could and did make a living independently, but the opportunities open to them were limited. A single woman could not hope to become rich if she was neither born to wealth nor married into it.

EIGHT

RELIGION

Asixteenth-century woman was expected to show love for God and to educate her family in their religion. Books written for women both at the time and earlier agreed that this was the most essential part of the woman's role. The Goodman of Paris starts his book by reminding his wife that 'you must gain the love of God and the salvation of your soul'[1] while Markham reminds his housewife right at the start of his book that she ought 'above all things, to be of an upright and sincere religion, and in the same both zealous and constant; giving by her example an incitement and spur unto all her family to pursue the same steps, and to utter forth by the instruction of her life those virtuous fruits of good living, which shall be pleasing both to God and his creatures.'[2]

Women of all classes became involved in the religious upheaval of the sixteenth century. At the top of society two women, the queens Mary I and Elizabeth I, were obviously at the centre of the religious debate, but as their role is discussed fully elsewhere it will not be discussed here.

The church was the bedrock of sixteenth-century society. The various festivals marked the seasons; its ceremonies blessed the stages of everyday life at christenings, weddings and funerals. At a time when death was never very far away it provided comfort in the hope that there was a better life to follow. Its physical presence was also a part of the landscape. In most towns there were not only churches but abbeys, nunneries, friaries and various other institutions, such as hospitals, which had church backing.

Today many people are brought up without any religious beliefs at all, which makes the depth of feeling that went into the sixteenth-century religious debate all the more difficult to understand. However, any religious belief which is strongly held affects all areas of life from how children are educated to how the family income is spent, and, of course, how authority is viewed. It was this last point which was all-important in the sixteenth century. Politics and religion were completely tied up together. Support for either Catholicism or Protestantism was strongly linked to supporting certain political views.

The situation was complicated by the fact that official policy on religion changed so frequently that sometimes people were unsure exactly what the 'official view' was. Sometimes even the monarch him or herself seems to have been unsure. Throughout the Middle Ages people had been used to obeying the lead given them by the parish priest, and following the practices which generations of their forefathers had followed. Now practices which everyone had been taught to observe for time out of mind, such as praying for the souls of the dead and lighting candles before the images of saints, became suspect. Familiar objects in the church came and went as official religious policy changed. Before discussing the woman's part in religion, therefore, some kind of overview of the religious changes of the period needs to be given.

At the beginning of the sixteenth century, England was most definitely a Catholic nation. There were still monks and nuns, just as there had been since the Middle Ages, and the monasteries do not seem to have been particularly in a state of decline.[3] There were calls for the reform of the Church, but these did not really affect the English Church until Henry VIII decided to rid himself of his first wife, Katherine of Aragon.

Henry VIII is usually seen as being the first English Protestant king, but this was certainly not the case. He was quite happy with Catholicism, and if the Pope had agreed to the annulment of his first marriage then it is unlikely that any significant reform would have come in his reign. The problem for Henry VIII was that those who were happy to see him made head of the English Church in place of the Pope tended to be those who also favoured further church reform, such as doing away with the worship of statues of saints and seeing that copies of the Bible were available in English so that people could study it for themselves. As a result, the reforms of Henry VIII's reign probably went further than the king had originally intended.

Thomas Cromwell, the minister who took Cardinal Wolsey's place as Henry VIII's right-hand man, certainly favoured change. While he was in power the reformers had the upper hand. It was he who oversaw the dissolution of the monasteries, and who actively encouraged a number of reforms such as the reduction of the number of saints' days observed and putting an end to pilgrimages. In March 1534 he made a memorandum to have substantial persons in every good town to discover 'all who speak or preach' against the reforms;[4] his postbag makes interesting reading as it shows how disputes over religious matters took place all over the country. Arguments between clergy and their congregations, or between neighbours, are all reported. For example, Thomas Coverley, vicar of Tysehurst, was in trouble in June 1538 for praising miraculous images and discouraging the reading of the Bible at a time when official policy was to encourage both these things. It is quite clear that even people right at the bottom were involved in the controversy surrounding the changes.

Those who spoke up for their beliefs were taking a risk. Even the wealthy and powerful had to be careful. By 1538 the reforms were being felt even in the English-run town of Calais. Cromwell was at the height of his powers. The wife of the governor of Calais, Lady Lisle, who seems to have favoured traditional religious views, received a letter from John Husee, the family's servant at the court. Lady Lisle, it seems, was holding to the old ways, burning candles before the images of saints and openly speaking in favour of conservative views. Mr Husee warns his mistress to be careful of how she worshipped:

I first protest with your ladyship not to be angry with me, but if it might be your pleasure to leave part of such ceremonies as you do use, as long prayers and offering of candles, and at some time to refrain and not speak, though your ladyship have cause, when you hear things spoken that liketh you not, it should sound highly to your honour and cause less speech . . .[5]

Even grand ladies like Lady Lisle could not consider themselves above trouble.

Cromwell fell out of favour and was beheaded in 1540. Official religious policy then became more conservative again, and we find those with more traditional views fighting back. The parson of Milton near Canterbury had removed an image of St Margaret because there had been a pilgrimage there, and pilgrimages were disapproved of by the reformers. On St Margaret's day in 1542 a certain John Cross, who had been cellarer at Christ Church, set up the image again, garlanded it with flowers and said mass in front of it.[6] He did this even though this was in the see of Canterbury, where Archbishop Thomas Cranmer was trying particularly hard to root out such practices.

The changes did not end with the death of Henry VIII in January 1547. His young son Edward became King. The regent was the Duke of Somerset, the brother of Edward's mother, Jane Seymour. Somerset was in favour of more reform, as was the young King who despite his youth took a great interest in religious affairs. During his short reign – he died in 1553 – England became a truly Protestant nation. At the end of Henry's reign the basic fabric of the Church as it had been at the end of the Middle Ages was still preserved in England. This was not the case by the time Edward died. A new prayer book came into force, the old images were done away with, the chantries where prayers were said for the souls of the dead disappeared – people must have been reeling with the many changes they saw. Many of the old, reassuring practices were gone.

A simple example of how deeply these reforms must have been felt is the removal from churches of many of the things which were believed to help women through childbirth. There are many records of girdles, such as Our Lady's girdle which was to be found at Westminster, and St Aelred's girdle which was kept at Rievaulx, for this purpose. As childbirth was a dangerous time, these must have been a considerable comfort for women during labour. The reformers saw such objects as heretical, as they led women to rely on the object rather than on God himself. To most ordinary women, the removal of such objects, which had after all been relied on by generations of mothers, must have seemed almost beyond comprehension.[7] Certainly their use must have been very widespread, as one of the promises a midwife had to make when she was officially licensed by her local bishop was not to use any such objects.[8]

The accession of Mary, Henry VIII's eldest daughter, as Queen in 1553 saw a reversal of policy. Mary realized that she could not put the clock back to how things had been before her father's reforms, but she did try to turn England back to being a Catholic nation. The images, and much of the church regalia which had disappeared under Edward, were now ordered back into the churches. Significant amounts of it had evidently been salted away by ordinary people, as it reappeared remarkably quickly. Doubtless many felt relief at the prospect of returning to the old, familiar ways.

Mary died in 1558, and with the accession of Elizabeth, policy was reversed yet again. Elizabeth's main concerns were that her religious settlement should be workable, and that it should be permanent. There was strong support for the reform movement not only amongst the wealthy and educated upper classes but also amongst the increasingly self-confident middle classes. It was, of course, impossible to find a religious settlement to please everyone, but a Protestant settlement seemed the best way and above all Elizabeth wanted to see an end to the chopping and changing that was so damaging to the country. For example, the images had to be not only removed this time, but, if they could be traced, destroyed. The Stonyhurst Salt, now in the British Museum, is an example of what happened to some of the jewels and plate that once adorned a church. England became Protestant again.

The religious debate of the sixteenth century was especially fierce as religion and politics were so firmly entwined. If you did not share the religious convictions of the government of the time, your loyalty was suspect. This was particularly the case at times of national emergency, such as the Spanish Armada of 1588, and in the 1590s when another Armada was expected. The atmosphere must have been rather similar to that in 1940–1, when a German invasion was thought to be imminent. Any Germans, regardless of their opinion of Hitler or how long they had been living in England, were regarded with suspicion. In the same way Catholics were suspected of being pro-Spain, and likely to be traitors. Protestants under Mary were considered likely to want to undermine the government. The attempt to put Lady Jane Grey on the throne must have added fuel to these suspicions.

It was impossible not to be affected by the changes so of course women as well as men became caught in the religious crossfire. Despite the limitations placed upon them, women with strong religious convictions were able to take an active part in supporting their religious views. Women were not, of course, allowed to have positions of authority in the Church. They could not be ordained as priests and neither could they preach. Their influence had to be more indirect, as they had to show suitable modesty, humility and obedience to their husbands. It was the women, though, who instructed the children in their religion, and many men who later got into trouble with the authorities for their religious views told those who examined them with pride that it was their mother or grandmother who had taught them. In Fox's *Acts and Monuments* for example, Thurston Littlepage tells his examiners that he had been taught the creed in English by his grandmother.[9]

Women were the organizers of households, and they were often well placed to help people, such as recusant priests, who needed food and shelter and some kind of base in England for their religious activities. Women could also fall foul of the authorities on religious matters just as men could; the records show women as well as men suffering persecution, and even death, for their faith, whether Catholic or Protestant.

The changes also affected women in that the nunneries were destroyed. Religion was the only career other than marriage open to the well-bred lady at the time. The last nunneries were suppressed in 1539 but until that time life in the nunneries continued very much as it had done for centuries.

The usual view is that the religious houses were on the decline and that the dissolution merely did away with a system that was already in decay. This does not seem to have been the case. The reports sent back to Cromwell on the state of the monasteries and nunneries were designed to show them in the worst possible light, so that he would have an excuse for doing away with them. Even if some houses were very badly off by this time they still seem to have been happily used by wealthy families for the education of their daughters. Two of Lord Lisle's daughters were entrusted to the Abbess of St Mary's convent in Winchester[10] and Robert Southwell wrote a report to Cromwell in 1537 of how he had seen one of Cromwell's granddaughters at Wilberfoss Nunnery in Yorkshire where she was being educated.[11] Certainly the nuns seemed no less well educated than ladies outside of the convent and there are various incidental references to them owning books.

Nuns all came from wealthy backgrounds. Any poor girl who wished to become a nun could only get as far as being a lay sister, who was in effect a servant. It was cheaper for a wealthy man to settle his daughter in a nunnery than to find a husband for her, but this did not mean that everyone who became a nun did so unwillingly. Women could not, after all, choose their husbands and religion could well have been a pleasant alternative. Inside the convent there were opportunities for responsibility without having to marry, as well as opportunities for study that a girl was unlikely to find elsewhere. In any case, girls who did become nuns were not forgotten by their families: they were often left legacies in wills of anything from furniture to jewellery and plate. Clearly the girls were not sent into religion purely so their families could be rid of them.

The closure of the nunneries must have been quite a loss for women. Those who wished to become nuns now had to go abroad. Many of the nuns certainly looked back with affection on their days in the convent: in the ten wills known to have been made by former Yorkshire nuns there are no fewer than twenty-four legacies left to their former sisters.[12]

The dissolution of the nunneries also left the former nuns badly off. Many, of course, had well-off families to return to but those who had to rely on the pensions given to them must have struggled. At Basedale in Yorkshire the prioress Elizabeth Roughton was given £6 13s and 4d at the dissolution but most of the nuns only had £1 per year to live on. It must have been hard for them to settle in the world too, as the nuns were not given permission to marry immediately and life as a single woman in the sixteenth century was not easy.[13]

The chance to live the religious life may have gone but the chance to play an active part in religion did not. The changes of the sixteenth century centred largely around the idea of being able to study the Bible, not to mention other religious works, for yourself. It was therefore very important that religious works should be translated into English, so as to reach as wide an audience as possible. Upper-class, educated women had both the ability and the time to do some of these translations. Translating religious works was just the kind of thing that was considered a suitable occupation for a lady, Vives recommends in his influential book *The Instruction of a Christian Woman.* One of the earliest of these translations was Margaret More-Roper's translation of Erasmus's *Devout Treatise upon the Pater Noster,* published in 1524. Her name does not actually appear upon the first edition. Instead the book is described as being 'turned into englishe by a young vertuous and well lerned gentylwoman'. Even though it was permissible for a woman to spend her time translating religious works, she had to be careful about publishing them. Even in the cause of religion a woman could not be seen to put herself forward.

The same spirit is seen in the publication of the Cooke sisters' work. They were the daughters of Anthony Cooke, who was tutor to Edward VI. Between them, four of the five sisters translated part of St Chrysostom, sermons by Bernadino Ochino, *The Apologia Ecclesiae Anglicanae or Answer in Defence of the Church of England* and *A Way of Reconciliation Touching the True Nature and Substance of the Body and Blood of Christ in the Sacrament.* The works which were published were produced in such a way as to suggest that the translator had no desire to be published, and had even been published against her will. The editor of the *Apologia* stresses that publishing was entirely his idea, as does the editor of Ochino's sermons.[14] In fact, none of the sisters seems to have been shy and unassuming – if anything, quite the reverse. It was simply important that they showed a token reluctance in order to have the works accepted.

Women were also important as patrons. This had been the case for centuries but in the sixteenth century, as views on religion changed, so did religious patronage. Margaret Beaufort, mother of Henry VII, was a very religious woman who supported a number of causes. She lived from 1443–1509, so it is not surprising that she supported many of the things that any conventional Catholic of the time would have done. For example, she founded many chantries, such as the one at Wimbourne Minster in Dorset, where prayers could be said for her soul after her death. Ironically, her grandson Edward VI later dissolved them. Other works that Margaret patronized proved to be more lasting. She was a patron of the new printing press, supporting Caxton, Wynkyn de Worde and Pynson. She also founded Christ's and St John's Colleges in Cambridge as the universities at the time were largely for the training of priests.

Anne Boleyn was another patron, although she favoured evangelical Protestantism.[15] The extent of Anne's patronage is difficult to judge as she was a rather controversial figure. After her death, many people were keen to show her as an utterly worthless adventuress, and it was unwise to say anything else. Equally, religious reformers such as Fox rather exaggerated her importance in order to flatter Elizabeth I. The truth is somewhere between the two extremes.

Anne was far more than a pretty woman who managed to catch the king's eye. She was certainly a very cultivated lady, having been educated at the glittering French court and also at that of Margaret of Austria in the Netherlands. She certainly read the Bible in English and French and a copy of the Bible in French which belonged to her still survives and is now in the British Library. She must have had a serious interest in Protestantism as she employed Hugh Latimer, something of a Protestant firebrand, as one of her chaplains. Anne helped and protected various people who got into trouble over their religious views both in England and abroad. William Latymer, who wrote a biography of Anne, states that she helped Nicholas Bourbon of Vandoevre who had been imprisoned in France for speaking against the Pope. She not only helped gain his release by obtaining letters from the King but also brought him to England and made him tutor to her nephew Henry Carey, Henry Norris and Thomas Howard.[16]

Providing work for men of particular religious persuasions was something that many well-off women were able to do. It might have been an unspectacular way of furthering a cause, but without suitable employment it would have been much harder for these men to go about spreading the word.

Katherine Parr, another of Henry's queens, was another patron of the reform movement. Protestant humanists such as Roger Ascham, John Aylmer, John Fox and Thomas Wilson all received appointments as tutors to the sons and daughters of royalty and nobility.[17] These men were to have considerable influence on their pupils, who included Lady Jane Grey, Princess Elizabeth and the future Edward VI. They also wrote a number of important works, such as Fox's *Acts and Monuments* telling of various Protestant Martyrs, a book which was reprinted for centuries. Ascham's book on education, *The Scholemaster*, advocated changes in education, encouraging the teaching of children through kindness and interest rather than through beatings. Society may have forbidden women such as Catherine to write original work of their own, but it certainly didn't stop them from helping others to do so.

Not all patronage was as spectacular. During Elizabeth's reign many recusant women were able to help the Catholic cause by providing places in their households for priests. Lady Anne Petre, who was a widow, used her home at Ingateston Hall as a base for Catholics. She employed as her steward John Payne, who was also a Catholic priest. He was eventually betrayed and executed for his faith in 1582 but only after he had been operating as a missionary from Ingateston for several years.[18]

Women such as Lady Anne were vital in keeping Catholicism alive in England during these years. Without places to stay, and, of course, places to hide in times of need, the priests could not have carried on their work. According to Richard Smith's *Life of Lady Montague*,[19] Lady Magdalene Montague, another widow, maintained three priests in her household, and even had a household chapel complete with all the necessary plate and vestments where a full mass with music was often said. According to Richard Smith there were sometimes 120 people at the service. Understandably, her house was known as 'Little Rome'. As if this were not enough, she also kept two houses near London Bridge which were used as safe houses for priests on their way in and out of London.

All the women discussed so far were wealthy and influential, and thus well placed to further their religious views. You did not have to be well-off to be able to support your views. Some very ordinary women were also able to make their public stance.

It was certainly not only the wealthy who harboured priests. Widows with their own homes, whether rich or poor, were especially well placed to help out but married women could help too. The Staffordshire Quarter Session Rolls[20] record Alice Tully, wife of Henry Tully, yeoman, who was 'a continual receiver' of two priests named Perton and Bounday. Alice Line, who was a widow, even kept three adjoining houses in London: one where she educated children and where she lived herself, another for priests to live in and another which was used as a rest house for Jesuits. She carried on this work for eight years before she was arrested and executed.

Sometimes the women's involvement was not as exciting as harbouring priests, but was no less important. Preachers needed somewhere to stay and women such as Mary Glover, the niece of Hugh Latimer, provided such practical assistance.[21] Mrs Statham, a London mercer's wife, was another such woman. She even looked after Hugh Latimer during an illness and he mentions her kind attentions in a letter to Cromwell.

During the years when the reformers were in favour this was merely friendly help but when reform was out of favour it was dangerous. In 1540 Mrs Statham was accused of supporting three men who were executed for their beliefs that year. Although Mary Glover herself survived, her husband Robert was burnt as a heretic in Coventry in September 1555 and Hugh Latimer was executed in Oxford in October of the same year. Being a known supporter of such men put a woman in a very precarious situation.

For a woman who wished to make a stance to support her religious views the fact that a married woman's property belonged not to her, but to her husband, worked to her advantage. Punishments such as fines and the confiscation of property simply meant nothing to married women, who in the eyes of the law owned nothing. Wives were therefore in a position to make their views known by not attending church, and by stating their views openly when brought to book of their offences, even if their husbands were not.

From 1559 onwards people were required by law to attend official Protestant church services. Those who did not attend were subject to fines and persistent offenders to the forfeiture of property. In the 1580s, as relations with Spain worsened, there was increasing pressure on those who did not conform, and in 1581 an 'Act to retain the Queen's Majesty's subjects in their due obedience' was passed. The Justices of the Peace, rather than the church courts, were now responsible for enforcing church attendance, and the matter was considered to be far more urgent than before.

From 1575 onwards the Earl of Huntingdon was the president of the Northern High Commission. He was very active indeed in trying to make sure that everyone went to church, so the proceedings at York give a good insight into the attitudes of both the recusant women, their husbands and also of the authorities.[22] By 1575 a hardcore of about forty determined recusant families had emerged. They came from a variety of backgrounds but some were from well-known families who even played a part in running the city. Lord Mayor Dinley's wife was one of those who refused to conform.

Some of the women were obviously expressing their own views and were going against their husband's wishes. Christopher Kinchingman had dragged his wife to church by force on one occasion and another, George Hull, had beaten his wife for her disobedience. Presumably both men disapproved of their wives' religious views. Others, it seems, were expressing their husbands' as well as their own views. A number of couples, such as the Geldarts and the Wellards were in conflict with the authorities for a long time. Often the husband would continue to attend church, so as to avoid forfeiting the family property, whilst the wife expressed the family views by not attending.

The women who were called before the authorities to answer for non-attendance were well able to express their reasons. Fifty-one of them were questioned in November 1576 and between them they covered most of the doctrinal issues at stake. One of the major points of disagreement between Catholic and Protestant was whether or not the consecrated bread and wine given at communion was merely symbolic of the flesh and blood of Christ, or whether it actually became the real thing; many of the women's answers revolved around this. Certainly the women do not seem to have been shy about expressing their views before men, however humble and submissive they may have been brought up to be.

These women, however, did not always get away without paying any penalty for their actions. Women could and were gaoled for their offences, and as Tudor gaols were not pleasant places to be, many died there. In 1594 it was reported that eleven women had died in Ousebridge gaol in York out of thirty imprisoned there over a fourteen-year period.[23]

The women were also in trouble if their husbands died, as the jointure settled on them at their marriage would then become their property. Two-thirds of this could be seized by the government, and the Exchequer Rolls of 1593–4 record sixty such seizures. This, however, does not seem to have stopped the women offending.

However high feelings ran regarding religion, the problem of the recusant wives was never really adequately solved. Towards the end of Elizabeth's reign Catholics were usually confined to staying within five miles of their home and a fine of £10, a considerable sum, was placed on the head of the household for every member of his family who did not attend church. In 1593 a bill was passed allowing for a husband to be sued jointly with his wife and a wave of recusant prosecutions followed, although the authorities soon backed off again. The government may have wanted religious conformity, but they realized that interfering in family life was a dangerous step. Essentially it was seen as a man's job to see that order was maintained in his family, and not the government's. The women's stance worked in the end.

In the religious upheavals women as well as men also paid the ultimate price and became martyrs. Fox's *Acts and Monuments* gives the most comprehensive account of the Protestant martyrs. It is, of course, openly biased in its view and very anti-Catholic, but even so it does show how the women were actively involved in furthering the cause. Sometimes the women are very much in the limelight, like Anne Askew, but others are mentioned almost in passing, sometimes suffering death together with their husbands. Others are not executed themselves but are still mentioned as having played an important part in their husband's work.

Anne Askew is the most famous of the Protestant martyrs, not only because Fox talks about her at length but also because she could have incriminated many important court ladies if she had not proved so strong under torture.[24] According to Fox, Anne unwittingly became part of a plot by Bishop Gardiner of Winchester, the Lord Chancellor, Wriothesley and others to discredit Queen Catherine Parr, who was, of course, a supporter of the reformist cause. Anne's refusal to name anyone even though she was put on the wrack thwarted the plot.

Anne also wrote an account of her first imprisonment, 'The First Examinacyon', which she finished shortly before she was burnt as a heretic at Smithfield. It is one of the few first-hand accounts written by a woman at the time. It shows a determined woman who had clearly thought out what her beliefs were and why. Anne was important to the reformers precisely because she was a woman. At the time, of course, women were seen as weak and by many as incapable of sound reasoning. Anne showed herself as anything but weak, and in her defence before the authorities showed herself capable of reasoning openly in public even with such an exalted man of the church as Bishop Bonner. She was seen as an example of the weak made strong by God, and certainly she refused to play the role of victim. This was no mean achievement for a woman at this time.[25]

The number of women who are mentioned almost in passing by Fox is quite considerable. They may not have been as famous as Anne but the sheer number of them shows how women were taking an active part in furthering their religious views despite the limitations placed on them. There was Alice Colins, wife of Richard Colins, who had such a good memory that she could recite 'much of the scriptures and other good books' and was often called upon to do just this for people who wished to study the Bible.[26] A certain J. Scrivener was forced by his oath to accuse not only John Barret, a goldsmith of London, but also his wife Joan and their servant, also called Joan, because Barret recited the Epistle of James in his house. Presumably they were studying the Bible together.[27] Elizabeth Young is mentioned as being in trouble for bringing forbidden books in English over from Emden and distributing them in London. Clearly the women were as fully involved in religious work as the men.[28]

For some women differences in religious views meant that they felt that they had no alternative but to leave their husbands. Anne Askew, whose parents had rather unwisely married her to an uneducated and firmly Catholic gentleman, eventually asked for a divorce and Elizabeth Bowes, who became John Knox's mother-in-law, became so estranged from her husband that she even followed Knox to Geneva.[29]

In religious matters, as in other areas, women were forced to take a back seat in not being allowed to be priests or to preach. However, they did make the most of the opportunities they had and, as in the case of the recusant wives, were even able to use the legal position of their sex to their own advantage. When they were forced into the spotlight on being called to account for their disobedience they showed themselves capable of sound argument and clear expression. This must have been an especial challenge to the women who had been taught not only to be humble and submissive but also to keep their opinions to themselves. The fact that so many of them acquitted themselves so well is a great tribute to them.

CONCLUSION

The ideal Tudor woman, according to the literature of the time, was the chaste, silent and obedient woman described in all the books full of advice on the organization of the home and family and on how a well-bred woman should behave. These books give the impression that Tudor women were quiet and humble, that they never voiced opinions in public, and that they gave way to their husbands in everything. All these books were written by men, and we have little evidence of what the women thought about this ideal. The recorded behaviour of women of the time suggests that they took a rather different approach in real life.

For one thing, the model of the chaste, silent and obedient woman was contradictory at a time when a woman was supposed to be able to manage a household and cope with business affairs. This must have meant dealing with men as equals at least part of the time. If they could bargain effectively with men over business deals they must have been far more formidable than the deportment books suggest. These women must have known their own minds and have been far more than the mere extension of their husband which they were in the eyes of the law.

There were a number of remarkable women who achieved a great deal despite the handicap of their sex. The Countess of Shrewsbury, Bess of Hardwick, climbed to the top by a series of marriages, and became one of the wealthiest women in England. She is most famous as the builder of Hardwick Hall, but she also built and furnished the Elizabethan house at Chatsworth, which was later pulled down to make way for the present building. She was far more than just an enthusiastic builder of houses, however, as she proved herself tough enough to stand up to her estranged fourth husband, George Talbot, Earl of Shrewsbury and, after he died, his son and heir. Much of the Talbot property remained in her hands despite the new heir's attempts to reclaim it.[1]

Catherine Willoughby, Duchess of Suffolk, married for the second time for love, even though she married rather beneath herself. She was also strong-minded enough to go abroad, under very difficult circumstances, when the religious situation under Queen Mary made it impossible for her and her family to stay in England and maintain their Protestant faith. This also meant the loss of her property, although fortunately for Catherine this was returned when Elizabeth came to the throne.

Margaret More-Roper's writings demonstrated that a woman could be every bit as intelligent as a man if she was given an equal education. This was especially remarkable at a time when there was a serious intellectual debate about the position of women. Were they capable of reason? Was it wise to educate such creatures? Were they capable of good moral behaviour without very strict supervision by a man, whether that man was their father or their husband? These were not questions asked only by a minority of men who were particularly embittered against women for some reason, but were questions seriously considered in academic circles.

The women considered above were all very wealthy, and in any age it is always easier for the rich to go against the norms of society. What about the women lower down the social scale? What did they think about being considered inferior beings? Women were not, as we have seen, given an opportunity to answer these debates openly in print, so it is hard to know what their response was. Most women probably did not concern themselves with the matter at all, as they were too busy with other things to pay much attention to a theoretical debate. Certainly a study of women's reading hardly suggests a rush of women trying to educate themselves through reading to prove the men wrong.[2]

The education of women was justified only on the grounds that reading and translating suitable moral works was a good way of keeping them occupied, and that it improved their moral judgement. In the sixteenth century the aim of education for both boys and girls was not only to improve their prospects of advancement, but also to improve their morals. It was thought that the study of the behaviour of great people of the past would inspire them to follow their example. It is for this reason that the educational writings of the time make so many references to the examples of history. The courtly conversation recorded in Castiglione's *The Courtier* is peppered with references to everyone from Alexander the Great to the Sabine women. Even the Goodman of Paris's prologue to his book is full of such references. '. . . You should be humble and obedient to him [i.e. your husband] after the example of Griselda,' and then goes on to cite various other examples of women from legend, the Bible and antiquity that she should follow in this respect.[3]

If reading could have such a powerful effect to the good, it also followed that it could set a bad example too if the wrong works were studied. The advice of men such as Vives was that women's reading material should be strictly limited by the men who supervised them. The women were not only to avoid certain classical works, such as Ovid, but were also to avoid romances such as Launcelot of the Lake or Tristan and Isolde.[4]

But what exactly did the women read? It is of note that the only book that Grace Sherrington seems really to have studied is Turner's *Herbal* and another book on surgery.[5] Lady Margaret Hoby's reading seems to have consisted entirely of religious works. If these two ladies are typical, then it shows just how unusual the sophisticated reading of the More girls and Lady Jane Grey was. Certainly most of the works published for women during the period 1475–1640 were practical or devotional works. It was only during the years 1573–82 that the number of books addressed to women increased noticeably. Even so, of the sixty-one titles which may be called women's literature published between 1573 and 1602 only twenty-one can be classified as fiction or some other form of recreational reading.[6] This suggests that women were not defying male advice as far as reading went.

Sixteenth-century women do not in general seem to have rebelled against the secondary position they held in society. As modern women looking back, this seems to us quite incredible, but this was a time when people were taught from earliest youth to accept authority and not to question. The women were simply living life as it had always been lived. This attitude becomes more understandable when you consider that even at the beginning of the twentieth century, at the time of the Suffragettes, there were many women of all classes who felt that involvement in politics was most unfeminine and that women didn't need the vote anyway.

Those who were most likely to be aware of the tensions caused by the restrictions placed on women were the wealthy and educated ladies who knew that they could hold their own against any man intellectually, and yet saw how they were never considered as equals by men. At least one of these women rebelled not by protest but by advising against education for women. Elizabeth Jocelyn in her prefatory letter to her *Mother's Legacy*, published in 1624, expresses her dying wish for her unborn child. If it is a girl, she wants it taught only the Bible, 'good housewifery, writing, and good workes' because 'other learning a woman needs not.'

Elizabeth herself had been educated by her grandfather, a professor of divinity at Cambridge. She had been taught foreign languages, history and poetry as well as Scripture. She gave her reasons for wanting to deny her daughter education as follows: 'Though I admire it in those whom God hath blest with discretion, yet I desire not much in mine owne, having seene that sometimes women have greater portions of learning, than wisdome, which is no better use to them than a main saile to a flye-boat, which runs it underwater.'[7]

Elizabeth clearly found the stresses of being an unusually well-educated woman too much. Even so, it never occurred to her to question the system that made her feel so out of place. Instead, it was easier to blame her family for giving her an 'unfeminine' education.

Other women in Elizabeth's situation were not overwhelmed by the position that their formidable education gave them, and instead made good use of it. They simply did not seem to have worried about the theory of their position compared to men. They knew that they had to use their influence privately and with a certain amount of discretion, and knew that it was certainly necessary to maintain, in public at least, a suitable air of humble obedience and submission to their husbands. Even working with these restrictions, they were able to profit by their education. The Cooke sisters are good examples of such women.[8]

All four sisters, as we have seen, had to appear very modest and reticent about having their translation work published. Their letters, however, reveal not only just how well educated they were but also how they were prepared to put that education to use in advancing their family's interests. With the family interests at stake, the public face of humility vanishes rather quickly.

All four women were married to important men. The eldest, Mildred, was the wife of William Cecil, the first Baron Burghley, who was so prominent in the reign of Elizabeth I. Anne was the wife of Nicholas Bacon, Lord Keeper of the Privy Seal. Elizabeth's first marriage was to Sir Thomas Hoby (who was himself the translator of Castiglione's *The Courtier*); and her second to Lord John Russell. Katherine was the wife of Sir Henry Killigrew, who was employed on various diplomatic missions by Elizabeth I. All the sisters also produced translations of religious works, which were referred to in Chapter Eight.

Well-bred and well-connected ladies like the Cooke sisters had considerable influence which friends and family expected them to use. Although convention caused them to show modesty in the publication of their works, the sisters showed no desire to hide their abilities when dealing with business. Elizabeth Cooke Hoby was happy to give her opinions to her brother-in-law, Lord Cecil, over a legal dispute involving her daughter. She even argued over legal precedent with him, and obviously expected to be taken seriously. Mildred is seen giving advice to a cousin, Sir William Fitzwilliam, who was Lord Deputy of Ireland. He was hoping to resign his position but Mildred wrote to him in Latin advising him to stay on a little longer. She also seems to have been very active in business around the Queen's wards. Cecil was master of the court of wards, a very lucrative post, and many people wrote to Mildred trying to obtain wardships. Anne was more interested in religion than politics, and she happily used her influence to help and protect reformist preachers. The Cooke sisters were certainly not powerless, despite being women.

Many middle-class women must also have felt far from powerless, even if their official position in the eyes of the law makes them sound so. They would have had at least one or two servants to manage, and if their husbands ran their own businesses it is likely that they were encouraged to play an active part in this. Women who were keeping the accounts, working in the shop and generally being included in discussions about business most likely gained a great deal of satisfaction from their daily life. The problem must have been that if your marriage was unhappy, your husband was in a position to make life very difficult for you, as Chapter Seven shows. Cases as extreme as that of Thomas Field, the London cordwainer who left his wife virtually nothing,[9] seem to have been unusual. The possibility of such things happening was always there in the background but many men must have seen their wives as valuable partners in running the business.

The women's letters that survive from the period do not suggest that the writers felt downtrodden in any way. The Paston women all come across as being strong characters, to whom their various menfolk looked for advice on all kinds of matters. They certainly do not restrict their advice to matters that might be thought properly to concern a women, such as advising on health and diet. Here is Margaret, writing to her husband John Paston I in 1448. She is preparing for an attack on one of the family properties at Gresham. She seems to have matters in hand:

Ryt wurchipful hwsbond, I recomawnd me to zu and prey zu to gete som crosse bowis and wyndacis to bynd them wyth, and quarell for zwr hwsis here ben so low that there may non man schete owt wyth no long bowe thow we hadde neuer so moche nede. I sopose ze xuld haue seche thyngis of Sere Jon Fastolf is ze wold send to hym. And also I wold ze xuld gete ij or iii schort pelle-axis to kepe wyth doris, and also many jakkys and ze may. . . .[10]

There is no question of it being unfeminine to get involved in such things. Margaret quietly organizes the defence of the property as best she may. It is of note that she was still only in her early to mid-twenties at the time.

Margaret expects her advice to be heeded not only by her husband, but also by other members of her family, even when they are fully grown. Here are her feelings on the loss of the Caister Castle, one of the family properties, to the Duke of Norfolk in 1469. She wrote to her son, Sir John Paston: 'And as for the yielding of Caistor, I suppose that Writtle has told you of the agreements by which it was surrendered. I would that this had been done before this time and then there would not have been so much harm done as there has been in various ways. For many of our well-wishers are put to loss for our sake . . .'[11] Margaret was clearly a woman who expected to be consulted fully on all the major issues concerning the family.

On a less pleasant note, her daughter Elizabeth Paston, whose marriage took some years to organize, suffered beatings at the hands of her mother, who seems to have suspected that she had some marriage plans of her own, rather than from any of the men of the family.

Margery Paston, wife of John Paston III, comes over as a less formidable character than her mother-in-law, Margaret Paston, but she also writes to her husband of business affairs. Fortunately, she never had to defend the family property from attack, but she had to involve herself in keeping the family in favour with the right people. Here she is writing of her intentions to speak to the Duchess of Norfolk on behalf of her husband in November, 1481: 'Item, ser, on Saturday last past I spacke wyth my cosyn Gornay, and he seyd if I wold goo to my lady of Norffolk and besech hyr good grace to be youre good and gracyous lady, she wold so be; for he seyd that one word of a woman shuld do more than the wordys of xx men . . .'[12]

Their marriage was very much a love match, and there is a touching postscript added to another letter written in November 1481: 'Ser, I prey you if ye tary longe at London that it will please [you] to sende for me, for I thynke longe sen I lay in your armes.'[13]

Slightly lower down the social scale, Sabine Johnson, although often apart from her husband John, was clearly very fond of him and was in turn held in high regard by him. She certainly did not take criticism of her housekeeping abilities lightly – the incident over her bread recorded in Chapter Five shows her to be a very spirited lady indeed. She also held her own in a family quarrel over money. Money was tight at the time, and her brother-in-law Otwell had replied angrily to her request for money. (Otwell, in London, normally kept Sabine supplied with money on behalf of his brother and business partner John, Sabine's husband, when John was in Calais.)[14] Sabine was far from being cowed by her brother-in-law's reaction. He soon found that she had a temper to match his own. She created such a fuss that Otwell remained offended for some time, and John had to tread carefully with both of them to mend the dispute. Sabine obviously felt no compunction to bow to either John or Otwell because they were men.

Honour Lisle, wife of Viscount Lisle, was very much the backbone of her family.[15] John Husee, the tireless family servant, was always careful to repeat in his letters to her all the business matters he had reported to Lord Lisle. She organized the whole family, treating her step-children in exactly the same way she treated her own children, and being quite inexhaustible in her efforts to forward the careers of all of them. When there was a dispute over the Lisle lands at Painswick in Gloucestershire it was Lady Lisle, not Viscount Lisle, who went to court to discuss the matter with no lesser person than Cromwell himself. Unfortunately, Lady Lisle was unsuccessful and ended up giving up her right to the land, but she certainly put up a good fight.[16]

These women clearly were not afraid of voicing their opinions, whatever the deportment books had to say on silence being a necessary quality in a woman. They also appear as being quite contented. Married, reasonably well-off women had, after all, plenty of outlets for their talents. They had so much to do that all skills could be used. Even talents that might not at first sight have been useful to a Tudor woman were needed. They had outlets for artistic skills; for example, in producing the elaborate sugar-work that was expected to be on the table when there were guests to be entertained and, of course, in their needlework.

The women who really suffered in the sixteenth century were those who never married, or poor women who were left widowed with children dependent on them. Society at the time did not really have a place for an independent woman. It was possible for them to make a living, but almost impossible for them to do much more than get by. What is most frustrating is that these are the women of whom we know least. The chances are that most of them could neither read nor write, and we have no letters or diaries left by them. They were not rich enough to buy books, so no books were written with them as an audience in mind. How they felt about life remains a mystery.

However the women felt about things, there is no doubt that their skills, whether acknowledged or not, were every bit as vital to the society of the time as those of their male counterparts. Certainly Tudor women would have understood more about the pressures of juggling the needs of a family with the pressures of work than most women of today.

NOTES

INTRODUCTION

1   Alison J. Carter 'Mary Tudor's Wardrobe', *Costume Society Journal* No. 18, 1984, p. 15
2   Barbara Winchester, *Tudor Family Portrait* (London, Jonathan Cape, 1955), p. 92
3   Roger Virgoe (ed.), *The Illustrated Letters of the Paston Family* (Guild Publishing, 1989), pp. 147–8, 161
4   I am indebted to Tom Campbell from the Victoria and Albert Museum for this information
5   Joyce Youings, *Sixteenth Century England* (The Pelican Social History of Britain series, Penguin Books, 1984), p. 133
6   Youings, *Sixteenth Century England*, p. 68
7   Youings, *Sixteenth Century England*, p. 89
8   See Chapter Seven
9   Youings, *Sixteenth Century England*, pp. 137–9
10 For a study of life in Aldgate, one of the poorer London parishes, see Thomas R. Forbes, *Chronicle from Aldgate* (New Haven and London, Yale University Press, 1971)
11 Youings, *Sixteenth Century*, England p. 340
12 See Chapter Two
13 Ralph A. Houlbrooke, *The English Family 1450–1700* (London and New York Longman, 1984), p. 136
14 For more information on Catherine Willoughby see Pearl Hogrefe, *Women of Action in Tudor England* (Iowa State University Press, 1977)
15 Winchester, *Tudor Family Portrait*, p. 269

16   See Chapter Six
17   *The Book of Nurture* is reprinted in Dr Furnivall and Edith
      Rickert (eds), *The Babees' Book Medieval Manners for the Young*
      (London, Chatto & Windus, 1923). The seating arrangements
      are on p. 71
18   See Muriel St Clare Byrne (ed.), *The Lisle Letters* (Penguin
      Books, 1985), section on 'Educating the Children'
19   See Chapter Seven
20   Winchester, *Tudor Family Portrait*, p. 224
21   'Family' at the time meant anyone who lived in your
      household. Pepys uses the word often but one example can be
      found in Robert Latham (ed.), *The Illustrated Pepys* (London,
      Book Club Associates, 1979), p. 104
22   For more information see David Loades, *The Tudor Court*
      (Bangor, Headstart History, 1992), sections on 'Politics' and
      'Religion'
23   See Chapter Eight
24   Richard Smith's '*Life of Lady Mary Montague*' is published as
      A.C. Southern (ed.), *An Elizabethan Recusant Household* (London
      and Glasgow, Sands and Co. Ltd, 1954)
25   See Chapter Two
26   Youings, *Sixteenth Century England*, p. 294
27   See Chapter Seven
28   Gervase Markham was the sixteenth/seventeenth-century
      version of a hack journalist and wrote a number of practical
      manuals. The one referred to in this book is *The English
      Housewife*, which was originally published in 1615. A
      modern version is available, edited by Michael R. Best and
      published by McGill-Queen's University Press, 1986. Thomas
      Tusser also wrote a variety of books but his best-known
      work is *Five Hundred Points of Good Husbandry* originally
      published in 1557. It is written in verse, which renders it
      more easily committed to memory. The quality of the verse
      is rather questionable but the book is a mine of information
      on everyday life at the time. It was reprinted, with an
      introduction by Geoffrey Grigson, by Oxford University Press
      in 1984.

Notes

CHAPTER ONE

1   Ralph A. Houlbrooke, *The English Family 1450–1700* (Longman Group, 1984), p. 63
2   Houlbrooke, *The English Family*, p. 82
3   Roger Virgoe (ed.), *The Illustrated Letters of the Paston Family* (London, Guild Publishing, 1989), p. 58
4   Pearl Hogrefe, *Tudor Women: Commoners and Queens* (Iowa State University Press, 1975), p. 17
5   F.J. Furnival (ed.), *Tell-Trothes New Yeares Gift* (London, N. Trüber and Co., 1876), p. 5
6   Richard Jones, *An Heptameron of Civil Discourses* (London, George Whetstone, 1582)
7   Virgoe (ed.), *Illustrated Letters of the Paston Family*, p. 99; plus letters associated with it
8   Houlbrooke, *The English Family*, p. 76
9   Houlbrooke, *The English Family*, p. 84
10 Houlbrooke, *The English Family*, p. 85
11 Houlbrooke, *The English Family*, p. 87
12 Right Revd E.C.S. Gibson (ed.), *The First and Second Prayer Books of Edward VI* (London, J.M. Dent & Sons Ltd, 1957)
13 Virgoe (ed.), *Illustrated Paston Letters*, p. 13
14 Houlbrooke, *The English Family*, p. 78
15 William Whately, *A Bride Bush, or A Direction For Married Persons Planely Describing the Duties Common to both and peculiar to each of them* (London, Thomas Man, 1619), p. 15
16 Hogrefe, *Tudor Women*, p. 14
17 Hogrefe, *Tudor Women*, p. 15
18 Dorothy M. Meads (ed.), *Diary of Lady Margaret Hoby* (London, George Routledge, 1930)
19 Barbara Winchester, *Tudor Family Portrait* (London, Jonathan Cape, 1955)

CHAPTER TWO

1   *Aristotle's Complete Masterpiece, Aristotle's Experienced Midwife,* and *Aristotle's Last Legacy* were all popular texts. The oldest edition of the *Masterpiece* is dated 1694 but in *Obstetrics and Gynaecology in Tudor and Stuart England* (London, Croom Helm,

1982) Audrey Eccles considers the information given in it to be much older.

2   F. Moriceau, *The accomplisht Midwife*, tr. H. Chamberlein (1673), p. 23, quoted from Audrey Eccles, *Obstetrics and Gynaecology in Tudor and Stuart England.*

3   See Chapter Six for explanation

4   Moriceau, *The accomplisht Midwife*, p. 231, quoted from Eccles, *Obstetrics and Gynaecology in Tudor and Stuart England.*

5   T.R. Forbes, *The Midwife and the Witch* (Yale University Press, 1966), see chapter entitled 'Chalcedony and Childbirth.'

6   T.R. Forbes, *The Midwife and the Witch*, as above

7   J Guillemeau, *Childbirth, or The Happy Delivierie of Women* (1612), p. 27

8   Patricia Crawford, 'The Construction and Experience of Maternity in Seventeenth Century England' in Valerie Fildes (ed.), *Women as Mothers in Pre-Industrial England* (London and New York, Routledge, 1990)

9   *The Private Correspondence of Jane, Lady Cornwallis* 1633–1644 (London, p. 85) quoted in Crawford, 'The Construction and Experience of Maternity'

12 Crawford, 'The Construction and Experience of Maternity', p. 53

11 Gervais Markham, *The English Housewife*, ed. M.R. Best (Quebec, McGill-Queen's University Press, 1986), p. 131

12 For a more complete discussion of this point see Adrian Wilson, 'The Ceremony of Childbirth and its Interpretation' in Valerie Fildes (ed.), *Women as Mothers in Pre-Industrial England*

13 Simon Thurley, *The Royal Palaces of Tudor England* (Yale University, 1993), p. 140

14 Muriel St Clare Byrne (ed.), *The Lisle Letters* (Penguin Books, 1985), pp. 306– 12

15 *The 1990 Demographic Handbook* (New York, United Nations, 1990)

16 As the civil registration of births and deaths was not made law until 1837, estimating figures such as maternal mortality is a problem before then. Estimates vary quite considerably for the sixteenth century.
    See R. Schofield 'Did the Mothers Really Die? Three Centuries of Maternal Mortality' in *The world we have gained*, ed. Lloyd

Notes

Bonfield, Richard M. Smith and Keith Wrightson (Oxford, Blackwell, 1986)

17   Guillemeau, *The Nursing of Children* (1612), p. 14

18   Wilson, 'The Ceremony of Childbirth'

19   For a full transcript of a sixteenth-century midwife's oath see Forbes, *The Midwife and the Witch*, p. 145

20   Alison Weir, *The Six Wives of Henry VIII* (London, Pimlico, 1992), p. 368

21   *The First and Second Prayer Books of Edward VI*, with introduction by Right Revd E.C.S. Gibson (London, J.M. Dent, 1957)

22   Carlson (ed.), *The Writings of Henry Barrow, 1587–1590*, quoted from William Coster, 'Purity, Profanity and Puritanism: the Churching of Women 1500–1700', in W.J. Sheils and Diana Wood (eds), *Women in the Church* (Basil Blackwell for the Ecclesiastical History Society, 1990)

23   Coster, 'Purity, Profanity and Puritanism', p. 384

24   Coster, 'Purity, Profanity and Puritanism', p. 383

25   A. Macfarlane (ed.), *The Diary of Ralph Josselin* (London, 1976), quoted from Wilson, 'The Ceremony of Childbirth'

26   Joyce Youings, *Sixteenth Century England* (Penguin Books, London, 1988), p. 372

27   Guillemeau, *The Nursing of Children*, p. 21

28   Eucharius Rosslin, *The Byrth of Mankynd*, tr. Richard Jonas (1540)

29   Guillemeau, *The Nursing of Children*, p. 24

30   R. Barret, *A Companion for midwives, childbearing women and nurses* (1699), quoted from Eccles, *Obstetrics and Gynaecology in Tudor and Stuart England*

CHAPTER THREE

1   Thomas Becon, *The Catechism*, ed. Revd John Ayre (Cambridge University Press, 1844)

2   Baldesar Castiglione, *The Book of the Courtier*, trans. George Bull (Penguin Classics, 1967) p. 218

3   *The Book of the Courtier*, p. 211

4   Heinrich Bullinger, *The Christen State of Matrimonye* (1541),

quoted from Suzanne W. Hull, *Chaste, Silent and Obedient* (San Marino, Huntingdon Library, 1982) p. 49

5 For more information on women academics in the sixteenth century see Margaret P. Hannay (ed.), *Silent but for the Word* (Ohio, Kent State University Press, 1985)

6 Muriel St Clare Byrne (ed.), *The Lisle Letters* (London, Penguin Books, 1985) p. 269

7 Quoted from Pearl Hogrefe, *Tudor Women: Commoners and Queens* (Iowa State University Press, 1975) p. 9

8 See Chapter Seven for more information

9 David Cressy's figures are quoted from Hull, *Chaste, Silent and Obedient*, p. 4. This book is a survey of books for women published in the sixteenth century and makes very interesting reading.

10 Many of Sabine's letters are published in Barbara Winchester, *Tudor Family Portrait* (London, Jonathan Cape, 1955)

11 Dorothy M. Meads (ed.), *Diary of Lady Margaret Hoby* (London, George Routledge and Sons, 1930)

12 Meads (ed.), *Diary of Lady Margaret Hoby*, introduction, also see comments in Hogrefe, *Tudor Women: Commoners and Queens*, p. 69

13 Winchester, *Tudor Family Portrait*, p. 178

14 Gervase Markham, *The English Housewife*, ed. Michael R. Best (Kingston and Montreal, McGill-Queen's University Press, 1986) p. 1 (frontispiece to 1615 edition)

CHAPTER FOUR

1 For information on the bathing arrangements in Tudor palaces see Simon Thurley, *The Royal Palaces of Tudor England* (Yale University Press, New Haven and England, 1993), pp. 167–71

2 Sir Hugh Plat, *Delightes for Ladies*, with introduction by G.E. Fussell and K.R. Fussell (Crosby Lockwood & Son Ltd, London, 1948), p. 90

3 Eileen Power (ed.), *The Goodman of Paris, A treatise on Moral and Domestic Economy by A Citizen of Paris, c. 1393* (George Routledge & Sons Ltd, London, 1928), p. 299

4 Plat, *Delightes for Ladies*, p. 89

5 Gervase Markham, *The English Housewife*, ed. Michael R. Best

(McGill-Queen's University Press, Kingston and Montreal, 1986), p. 170

6 Alison Weir, *The Six Wives of Henry VIII* (Pimlico, 1992), p. 368

7 Dorothy Hartley, *Water in England* (MacDonald & Co, London, 1964), pp. 346–8

8 John Gerard (enlarged by Thomas Johnson), *The Herbal, or General History of Plants* (1633 edition, Dover Publications Inc, New York, 1975), p. 1116

9 Power (ed.), *The Goodman of Paris*, p. 174

10 Thomas Tusser, *Five Hundred Points of Good Husbandry*, with intro by Geoffrey Grigson (Oxford and New York, Oxford University Press, 1984) p. 116

11 Ibid.

12 Power (eds.), *The Goodman of Paris*, p. 213

13 Ibid.

14 Richard Jones, *An Heptameron of Civil Discourses* (London, George Whetstone, 1582)

15 Hartley, *Water in England*, pp. 292–4

16 Celia Fiennes, *The Journey of Celia Fiennes*, quoted in Caroline Davidson, *A Woman's Work is Never Done* (1982)

17 *A Collection of Ordinances and Regulations of the Royal Household from Edward III to William III* (London III, Miscellaneous Institutions, 1790), p. 215

18 Hartley, *Water in England*, p. 290

19 Hartley, *Water in England*, p. 324

20 John Stow, *The Anals or General Chronicle of England*, ed. E. Hawes (London, 1615), p. 86

21 Philip Stubbes, *The Anatomie of Abuses* (London, 1583), pp. 22–3

22 Gerard, *The Herbal, or General History of Plants*, p. 835

23 Leonard Mascall, *A Profitable Book declaring dyvers approoved remedies to take out spottes and staines in silkes, velvets, linnnen and woollen clothes* (London, 1583). It also includes information on dyeing and how to soften iron and steel, amongst other things.

24 Mascall, *A Profitable Book*, fol. 13

25 John Russell, *The Book of Nurture*, in Dr F.J. Furnivall (ed.), *The Babees Book* (Ballantyne Press, 1923), p. 66

26 Power (ed.), *The Goodman of Paris*, p. 214

27 Mascall, *A Profitable Book*, fol. 11

28 Power (ed.), *The Goodman of Paris*, p. 215

29 I have been unable to find out exactly what 'Mertum Cudum' was. I believe it to be some kind of ground mineral

30 John Partridge, *The Treasury of Commodious Conceites* (London, 1586), cap. 84

31 Mascall, *A Profitable Book*, fol. 6

32 Mascall, *A Profitable Book*, fol. 9

33 Partridge, *The Treasury of Commodious Conceites*, cap. 85

34 Mascall, *A Profitable Book*, fol. 6

35 Mascall, *A Profitable Book*, fol. 2/3

36 Tussec, *Five Hundred Points of Good Husbandry*, p. 169

CHAPTER FIVE

1 The Johnson Family letters, quoted from Barbara Winchester, *Tudor Family Portrait* (Jonathan Cape, 1955)

2 Hilary Spurling (ed.), '*Elinor Fettiplace's Receipt Book*' (Penguin Books, 1986)

3 Elizabeth David, *English Bread and Yeast Cookery* (Penguin Books, 1977)

4 *Early 17th Century Prices and Wages* (Living History Reference Books Series, Stuart Press)

5 A wealth of information about banquets and 'banquetting stuffe' can be found in *Banquetting Stuffe*, edited by C. Anne Wilson (Edinburgh University Press)

6 Thomas Tusser, *Five Hundred Points of Good Husbandry*. This is a long poem, written in the fifteenth century, giving hints on running a household and small holding. The quality of the verse is questionable, but it does provide an interesting insight into running a household at this time.

7 The Johnson Family letters, quoted from Winchester, *Tudor Family Portait*

8 C. Anne Wilson, *Food and Drink in Britain* (Constable and Co.)

9 Spurling (ed.), *Elinor Fettiplace's Receipt Book*

10 Wilson, *Food and Drink in Britain*

11 'Fifteenth Century Schoolbook', quoted from Margaret Wade

Labarge, *A Baronial Household of the Thirteenth Century* (Harvester Press, 1980)

12 Gervase Markham, *The English Housewife*, first published in 1615, edition used here edited by M.R. Best (McGill-Queen's University Press, 1986)

CHAPTER SIX

1   This table is reproduced from S.E. Lehmberg, *Sir Thomas Elyot, Tudor Humanist* (University of Texas Press, 1960), p. 134

2   Sir Thomas Elyot, *The Castel of Helth* (British Library Catalogue no C.108 aaaa.19)

3   Elyot, *The Castel of Helth*

4   Gervase Markham, *The English Housewife*, ed. M.R. Best (McGill-Queen's University Press, 1986), Chapter One, p. 10

5   The *Castel of Helth*, quoted this time from W.S.C. Copeman, *Doctors and Disease in Tudor Times* (Wm Dawson & Sons, 1960)

6   Arnold of Villanova, quoted from Copeman, *Doctors and Disease in Tudor Times*

7   Thomas Hill, *The Gardener's Labyrinth, the First English Gardening Book*, edited by Richard Mabey (Oxford University Press,1987) p. 66

8   Markham, *The English Housewife*, Chapter One, p. 209

9   Copeman, *Doctors and Disease in Tudor Times*

10 Quoted from Copeman, *Doctors and Disease in Tudor Times*

11 Copeman, *Doctors and Disease in Tudor Times*

12 Markham, *The English Housewife*, Chapter One, p. 8

13 B. Ehrenreich and D. English, *Witches, Midwives and Nurses. A History of Women Healers* (New York, Feminist Press, 1973)

14 Ehreneich and English, *Witches, Midwives and Nurses*

15 *The Paston Letters*, quoted from *The Illustrated Letters of the Paston Family*, ed. Roger Virgoe (Guild Publishing, 1989) p. 278

16 *The Paston Letters*, this time quoted from M.J. Hughes, *Women Healers in Medieval Life and Literature* (New York, Books for Libraries Press, 1968)

17 Eugene Mason (trans), *Aucassin and Nicolette and other Medieval Romances and Legends* (Everyman, J.M. Dent & Sons, 1949), p. 27

18 Thomas Rogers Forbes, *Chronicle from Aldgate. Life and Death in Shakespeare's London* (Yale University Press, 1971), p. 227
19 Wilfred Blunt and Sarah Raphael, *The Illustrated Herbal* (Frances Lincoln, 1979)
20 Blunt and Raphael, *The Illustrated Herbal*
21 Sir Hugh Plat, *Delightes for Ladies*, with introductions by G.E. Fussell and K.R. Fussell (Crosby Lockwood and Son Ltd, 1948), p. 66
22 Plat, *Delightes for Ladies*, p. 63

CHAPTER SEVEN

1   For more details about the London silk women see Marian K. Dale 'The London Silk women of the Fifteenth Century', *Economic History Review* Vol 4 (1933)
2   Dale, 'The London Silk Women', p. 324
3   Dale, 'The London Silk Women', p. 325
4   Dale, 'The London Silk Women', p. 333
5   Dale, 'The London Silk Women', p. 328
6   Kay E. Lacey, 'Women and work in Fifteenth and Sixteenth Century London' in Linsey Charles & Lorna Duffin (ed.), *Women and Work in Pre-Industrial England* (Croom Helm, 1985)
7   W. Prideau, *Memorials of the Goldsmiths' Company, London 1576–7*, quoted in Lacey, *Women and work in Fifteenth and Sixteenth-Century London*, p. 48
8   William Herbert, *The History of the Twelve Great Livery Companies of London* (London, 1836/1837), p. 466
9   Vivian Brodsky, 'Widows in Late Elizabethan England', in Lloyd Bonfield, R.M. Smith and K. Wrightson (ed.) *The World We Have Gained* (Basil Blackwell, 1986)
10 Amy Lucy Eridson in her introduction to Alice Clarke, *The Working Life of Women in the Seventeenth Century*, p. xxx. See also Pearl Hogrefe, *Tudor Women: Commoners and Queens* (Iowa State University Press, 1975), p. 87
11 Brodsky, 'Widows in Late Elizabethan London', p. 123
12 Barbara Winchester, *Tudor Family Portrait* (Jonathan Cape, 1955), pp. 84–5

Notes

13 For more information on sixteenth-century Salisbury see Sue Wright, 'Charmaids, Huswyfs and Hucksters: The Employment of Women in Tudor and Stuart Salisbury' in Lacey, *Women and Work in Pre-Industrial England*

14 Sub-Dean's Wills, 1618, Wiltshire Record Office, quoted from Sue Wright, 'Charmaids, Huswyfs and Hucksters', p. 113

15 Wright, 'Charmaids, Huswyfs and Hucksters', p. 109

16 Salisbury Corporation Archives 1/252, quoted in Wright, 'Charmaids, Huswyfs and Hucksters'

17 Wright, 'Charmaids, Huswyfs and Hucksters', p. 103

18 J. Pound (ed.), *The Norwich Census of the Poor, 1570* (Norfolk Records Society xi, 1971) p. 55, quoted in Michael Roberts, 'Images of Work and Gender' in Lacey, *Women and Work in Pre-Industrial England*

19 Roberts, 'Images of Work and Gender', p. 127

20 Dorothy M. Meads (ed.), *The Diary of Lady Margaret Hoby 1599–1605* (George Routledge and Sons Ltd, London, 1930), introduction

21 Alice Clarke, *The Working Life of Women*, p. 107

22 Norwich Records, Vol. 1, p. 378, quoted in Clarke, *The Working Life of Women in the Seventeenth Century*, p. 103

23 Quoted from Clarke, *The Working Life of Women*, p. 99

24 Brodsky, 'Widows in Late Elizabethan England', p. 144

25 Herbert Heaton, *The Yorkshire Woollen and Worsted Industries* (Oxford Historical & Literary Studies, Vol. 10, Oxford, 1920), p. 95

26 For a more detailed explanation of the legal position of women in the sixteenth century see Lacey, 'Women and Work in Fifteenth Century London'

27 Sixteenth-century commentator quoted in Lacey, 'Women and Work in Fifteenth and Sixteenth Century London', p. 41

28 Dale, 'The London Silk Women', p. 329

29 Clarke, 'The Working Life of Women', pp. 221–3

CHAPTER EIGHT

1 Eileen Power (ed.) *The Goodman of Paris. A treatise on Moral and Domestic Economy by A Citizen of Paris 1393* (George Routledge & Sons Ltd, London, 1928), p. 43

2 Gervase Markham, *The English Housewife*, ed. Michael R. Best (McGill-Queen's University Press, Kingston and Montreal, 1986), p. 5

3 Anyone with an interest in sixteenth-century religion should read Eamon Duffy, *The Stripping of the Altars* (Yale University, 1992). This gives a very good account of the religious changes which took place, and also explains how Christianity was observed at popular level in England during the period.

4 Duffy, *The Stripping of the Altars*, p. 385

5 Muriel St Clare Byrne (ed.), *The Lisle Letters* (Penguin Books, 1985) p. 383

6 Duffy, *The Stripping of the Altars*, p. 440

7 See Duffy, *The Stripping of the Altars*, p. 384 for details of some of these girdles

8 See Thomas Forbes, *The Midwife and the Witch* (Yale University, 1966), p. 139 onwards for details of midwives' oaths. In 1584 an oath taken at the direction of the Bishop of Chester specified that the midwives were not to use 'any witchcraft, charmes, relics or invocation to any saint in the time of travail.'

9 John Fox, *Acts and Monuments* (9th edition, printed in London for the Company of Stationers, 1684), vol II, p. 29

10 Byrne (ed.), *The Lisle Letters*, p. 132

11 Claire Cross, 'The Religious Life of Women in Sixteenth Century Yorkshire' in W.J. Sheils and Diana Wood (ed.), *Women in the Church* (Ecclesiastical History Society, Basil Blackwell, 1990), p. 309. See whole article for more information on sixteenth-century nuns in Yorkshire.

12 Cross, 'The Religious Life of Women', p. 315

13 Cross, 'The Religious Life of Women', p. 314

14 For more details about the Cooke sisters see 'The Cooke Sisters: Attitudes toward Learned Women in the Renaissance' in Margaret P. Hannay (ed.), *Silent but for the Word* (Kent, Ohio, The Kent State University Press 1985)

15 Maria Dowling, 'Anne Boleyn as Patron' in David Starkey (ed.), *Henry VIII, A European Court in England* (London, Collins & Brown in Association with the National Maritime Museum, 1991), p. 107

16 Dowling, 'Anne Boleyn as Patron', p. 110. See also John N. King, 'Patronage and Piety: The Influence of Catherine Parr', p. 44 in Hannay (ed.), *Silent but for the Word*

17   King, 'The Influence of Catherine Parr', p. 44

18   Vatican Congregation of Rites, *The Canonization of Blessed Martyrs, Archdiocese of Westminster* (Vatican, Polyglot Press, 1968), p. 179 and 189

19   A.C. Southern (ed.), *An Elizabethan Recusant Household* (London and Glasgow, Sands and Co., 1954). This consists largely of Richard Smith's *Life of Lady Magdalene Montague*. Richard Smith lived in Lady Montague's household and so knew her first hand, although the *Life* is very idealized.

20   *Staffordshire Quarter Rolls II: 1590-93* (Stafford Record Society, Staffordshire Historical Collections), quoted in Marie B. Rowlands, 'Recusant Women 1560–1640', p. 157 in Mary Prior (ed.), *Women in English Society 1500–1800* (1985)

21   See Susan Wabuda, 'Shunamites and Nurses of the English Reformation: The Activities of Mary Glover, Niece of Hugh Latimer', in Sheils and Wood (ed.), *Women in the Church* for more information on these women.

22   See Rowlands, 'Recusant Women', section on 'Recusant Women and the Law' for more information

23   Rowlands, 'Recusant Women', p. 152

24   For Fox's account of Anne see *Acts and Monuments*, vol II, pp. 483–90

25   For a detailed criticism of Anne's '*Examinations*' see Elaine V. Beilin, 'Anne Askew's Self Portrait in the "Examinations"' in Hannay (ed.), *Silent but for the Word.*

26   *Acts and Monuments*, Vol II, p. 37

27   *Acts and Monuments*, Vol II, p. 29

28   *Acts and Monuments*, Vol III, p. 764

29   For more information on Elizabeth Bowes see Christine M. Newman 'The Reformation and Elizabeth Bowes: A Study of a Sixteenth Century Northern Gentlewoman' in Sheils and Wood (ed.), *Women in the Church*

CONCLUSION

1   For more information on some of the prominent women of the sixteenth century see Pearl Hogrefe, *Women of Action in Tudor England* (Iowa State University Press, 1977)

2   For a review of books published for women see Suzanne W. Hull, *Chaste, Silent and Obedient* (Huntington Library, San Marino, 1982)

3   Eileen Power (ed.), *The Goodman of Paris* (London, George Routledge & Sons Ltd, 1928), p. 44

4   Valerie Wayne, 'Some Sad Sentence: Vives' Instruction of a Christian Woman', p. 20 in Margaret P. Hannay (ed.), *Silent But for the Word* (Kent State University Press, 1985)

5   See introduction to Dorothy M. Meads (ed.), *Diary of Lady Margaret Hoby* (London, George Routledge & Sons, 1930), pp. 49–50

6   Hull, *Chaste, Silent and Obedient*, pp. 6–7

7   See Mary Ellen Lamb, 'The Cooke Sisters: Attitudes toward Learned Women in the Renaissance' in Hannay (ed.), *Silent but for the Word*, p. 114

8   Ibid.

9   See pp. 104–5

10 Norman Davis (ed.), *The Paston Letters and Papers of the Fifteenth Century* (Oxford University Press, 1971), p. 226, The 'quarell' mentioned are bolts for cross-bows (or 'crosse bowis' as Margaret spells it).

11 Roger Virgoe (ed.), *The Illustrated Letters of the Paston Family* (Guild Publishing, 1989), p. 190

12 Davis (ed.), *The Paston Letters and Papers*, p. 665

13 Ibid.

14 Barbara Winchester, *Tudor Family Portrait* (London, Jonathan Cape, 1955), pp. 95–100

15 Muriel St Clare Byrne (ed.), *The Lisle Letters* (Penguin Books, 1985). See pp. 45–9 for an overview of Lady Lisle's character

16 Ibid., section on Estate and Legal Business

INDEX

A Way of Reconciliation Touching . . .,
  126
abortion, 20
academic ability, attitudes to in
  women, 34–7
Accomplisht Midwife, The, 17
Act to retain the Queen's Majesty's
  subjects in their due obedience,
  1581, 131
Acts and Monuments, John Fox, 123,
  133
aetites, 17
Aldgate, London, 94
ale, 74–6
ammonia, 55
Anatomie of Abuses, Philip Stubbs, 56
Andrew Boorde, 83, 85
Annals, John Stow, 55
Apologia Ecclesiae Anglicanae, 126
apothecaries, 86, 87
apprentices, 100–02, 104, 106–7
Aragon, Katherine of, validity of
  marriage debated, 12–13
Aristotle's Masterpiece, 16
Arnold of Villanova, 82
arsenic, 59
Ascham, Roger, 128
Askew, Anne, 134–5
Asprella, 50
astrology, 82–4
Atkinson, Nicholas, 106

Avicenna, 28, 91
Aylmer, John, 128

Bab, Grace, marriage of daughter, 8
Bacon, Nicholas, 142
Banckes Herbal, 95
banns, 10
banquets, 69
barber-surgeons, 88
Bargrave, Dr, Dean of Christchurch,
  18
Barlow, Robert, 14
Basedale, Yorkshire 125
Basset, Anne, 40
Basset, Katherine, 40
Bay of Bourgeneuf, 72
Beaufort, Margaret, 127
bedding ceremony, 13
Bedford, Countess of, 19
beer, 74–6
belladonna, 90
Beverley, Yorkshire, 104
Bezoar stone, 84
black bullaces, 77
bleaching, 54–5
Boleyn Anne
  as patron, 127–8
  lying in of, 21
  marries Henry VIII, 11
Bonaventura, Thomasina, 13
Book of the Courtier, 35

Book of Nurture, John Russell, xvi, 58
books, xx
Boorde, Andrew, 74, 83
Bowes, Elizabeth, 135
bread, 64–6
brewing, 74–6
Bride Bush, A, 13
buck tub, 53
Burdon, Robert, 4
Burnaby, Thomas, 13
butter, 70–1
Byrth of Mankynd, The, 27, 28–9

Caister Castle, 145
Calais, 119
Calle, Richard, 12
Cannock Wood, 53
Carey, Henry, 128
Castel of Helth, The, 80, 95
Catechism, The, Thomas Becon, 31
caudle, 22
Cavendish, Sir William, 14
Cecil, William, 143
ceremony, wedding, 9–10
chantries, 32, 121, 127
charmaids, 108
Chatsworth, 138
cheese, 70–2
Childbirth, or The Happy Deliverie of Women, 18
children
    attitudes of parents to, xx, xxvi–vii
    attitudes to parents, xxiii
    feeding of the very young, 27, 29
Christ's College, Cambridge, 127–30
Christ's Hospital, 94
Christen State of Matrimonye, The, 36
christening, 24–5
churching, 25–6
cider, 76
Clare, Elizabeth 3
claret, 76
Clothworker's Company, 104
Colins, Alice, 135
colour, xi

Companion for Midwives, A, 30
confectionery, 68–9
Cooke sisters, 38, 126, 142–3
Cornwallis, Lady Jane, 19
Council of Tours, 85
Council of Trent, 11
Coverley, Thomas, vicar of Tysehurst, 119
crab applies, 74
Cranmer, Thomas, 120
cream, 71
Cromwell, Thomas, xviii, 118, 119, 120
Cross, John, ex-cellerar of Christ Church, 120
Cyprus
    wine from, 76

dairying, 70–1
damsons, 77
dancing, 37–38
Dashepener, John
    marriage settlement of, 9
De Humain Corporis Fabrica, 87
De' Medici, Guiliano, 35
Deacon, Elizabeth, 107
Delights for Ladies, 47, 97
Devout Treatise upon the Pater Noster, 126
Diary of Lady Margaret Hoby, 40–1
Dietary of Health, Andrew Boorde, 74–5
Dioscorides, 18
distilling, 97
Dodeous, 96
domestic service, 108
Drapers gild, 103
drying the wash, 55
Duke of Urbino, 35
Dutch rushes, 50

eagle stone, 17
Ealing, 107
Edward VI
    christening of, 24

Index

cleanliness of nurseries, 48
religious views of, 120
elecompane roots, 58
Elisabetta Gonzaga, 35
Elizabeth I
religious views of, 122
Elyot, Sir Thomas, 81, 82, 95
English Housewife, The, 20, 45, 48,
  62, 67, 71, 77, 81–2, 84, 89,
  97, 116
ergot, 90

femme sole, 113
Fettisplace, Lady Elinor, 64
Field of the Cloth of Gold, 64
Field, Thomas, cordwainer, 111
Fiennes, Celia, 53
First Examinacyon, The, 134
First Prayer Book of Edward VI, 11
fish, 73
Five Hundred Points of Good Husbandry,
  51, 61, 70
flies, control of, 51
four humours, the, 80–2,
Fox, John, 128
fuller's earth, 60
furs, maintenance of, 59

Galen, 79,
Gall, Henry, 13
Gardener's Labyrinth, The 83
gardens, xi
Gardiner, Bishop of Winchester, 134
Gerard, John, 96
Gerard's *Herbal*, 50, 56–7, 96
Geynes, Dr John, 85
gilds
silk women, 100, 101, 102
generally, 102–4
Glapthorn Manor, x, 63
Glover, Mary, 130
godparents, 24–5
Goodman of Paris, 50, 51, 58, 116,
  139–40
grease, removal from clothes, 60

Gresham, 144
Grey, Lady Jane, 122, 128
Gunter, Mary, 107

Hamblyn, Mistress, 43
Hampton Court Palace, 46
Hardwick Hall, 138
Hardwick, Bess of, 13, 138
Harris, Anne, laundress to Henry
  VIII, 54
hartshorn, 84
Henry VIII
bathrooms of, 46
faithful to friends, 39
female servants of, 108
laundress of, 54
marries Anne Boleyn, 11
religious views of, 118–20
tapestries, xi
Heptameron of Civil Discourses, An,
  7, 52
Hill, Thomas, 83
Hoby, Lady Margaret, 15, 43
Hoby, Sir Thomas, 142
Holme, Dionisia, merchant, 104
hops, 74
horse bread, 65
hours of work, xxi
Howard, Thomas, 128
Huntingdon, Earl of, 131
Husee, John, 37, 40, 119
Hypocrates, 79

incomes
gentlemen, xi
labourers, xii
shipwright, xi
Ingateston Hall, 129
Innocent III, Pope, 85
Instruction of a Christian Woman, The,
  37, 126
Itinerary of John Leyland, 110
ivory, 84

Jocelyn, Elizabeth, 141–2

Johnson
  Henry, xviii
  John, 7, 142, 63
  Otwell, xviii, xv, 133
  Sabine, 15, 42, 44, 63–4, 70, 78, 146
Johnson, Thomas, 96
jointure, 8
Jones, Richard, 7
Josselin, Jane, 26

Killigrew, Sir Henry, 142
Knollys, Roger, 4
Knox, John, 135

La Belle Iseult, 93
laces, 100
Langton, Jane, silk woman, 102
Latimer, Hugh, 128, 130
Latymer, William, 128
lavender, 59
Laycock Abbey, 43
laying the buck, 53
legal position of women, 112–13
Lent, 73
lettuce, 81
licences for doctors, 89
Life of Lady Montague, xx, 120
Line, Alice, 130
linen, undergarments, 52
linen, washing of, 52–4
Lisle
  Lady Honour, 21, 119–20, 146–7
Littlehampton, 9
Littlepage, Thurston, 123
London
  aldermen's widows of, 104
  conduits run with wine, 24
  literacy rates, 41
  population of, xii
  recusants in, 130
love, attitudes to, 6
lying in, 21–5

magic, 84

maid of honour, 40
Malmesbury, 110
Malmsey, 76
malt, 75
manchet, 66
marriage negotiations, 4–5
marriage settlements, 7, 8–10
marriage vows, 9–10
marriage, age at, 1–2
marriage, validity of, 10–13
Mary I
  dress, cost of, ix–x
  betrothal to Dauphin, 2
  education of, 34–35
  religious views of, 121–2
maslin, 66
May Day, 71
mead, 76
medical theories, 79–85
Merthum Cudum, 59
Milton, 120
monasteries, 124
Mones, Lewys
  wedding of, 10
Montague, Lady Magdalene, xx, 120
More-Roper, Margaret, 34, 138
Moriceau, 17
mortality rate, maternal, 22
mortality, infant, 27
Morte Darthor, Thomas Mallory, 93
moth, precautions against, 58
Mother's Legacy, 141

Needles Excellency, The, xxiii
Nicholson, Peter
  death of, 94
Nicolette, 93
Norris, Henry, 128
Norwich, 102, 104, 107, 109
Norwich Census of the Poor, 107
Norwich weavers, 109
nunneries, 124–5
nunneries, dissolution of, 124
nursing, 94–5
Nursing of Children, The, 28

ak of Jerusalem, 77
Ochino, Bernadino, 116, 126
orange peel, 58
Our Lady's girdle, 121
Ousebridge gaol, York, 133
ovens, 65

Painswick, 147
Paracelsus, 91
Parr, Katherine
  as patron, 128–9
Paston
  Elizabeth, 3, 145
  John Paston III, 92
  Margaret, 93, 145
  Margery (later Calle), 12
  Margery, (nee Brews), 7, 92, 145
Payne, John, 129
pedlars, 110
Percival, Sir Thomas, 13
perfumes, 47–8
Petre, Lady Anne, 129
pickling, 74
Pliny, 18
Plumpton, Sir William, 11
population, xii
population, mobility of, xiii
pottage, 64
prayer book of Edward VI, 9
precedence, xvi
pregnancy
  numbers of per woman, 16–18
  pre-natal care, 15–16, 17
  tests for, 16–17
  women's feelings about, 18–19, 40
Preston, 26
Profitable Book Declaring Dyvers
    Approved Remedies, 59
psychological problems, 81

Rawe, Jane, merchant, 104
reading, restriction of women's, 36,
    37, 140
Recorde, Robert, 86
regraters, 110

remarriage, 14–15
Rievaulx, 120
Rokes, Thomas
  marriage of child, 7
Romney, 76
roses, 93
rosewater, 93
Roughton, Elizabeth, 125
Royal College of Physicians, 89
ruffs, 55–6
Russell, Lord John, 142
Russia, 73
Rutland, Lady, 40

Salisbury, 102, 105–6, 108
Salisbury Corporation Archives, 107
sallets, 67–8
salt, 72
salting meat, 72
Scandinavia, 73
Scholemaster, The, 128
scouring, methods of, 50
servants, attitudes to, xvii–xviii
Seymour, Jane
  death of, 23
shave-grass, 50
Sherrington, Grace (later Lady
    Mildmay), 43–4
silk women, 100–2
sinks, 49–50
small beer, 75
soap, household, 53–4, 60
soap, toilet, 47, 59–60
soapwort, 59–60
Somerset, Duke of, 120
Sorbonne, 83
Spanish Armada, 122
spinning, 109
St Aelred's girdle, 121
St Bartholomew's Hospital, 94
St Chrysostom, 126
St Isidore, 18
St John's College, Cambridge, 127
St Lose, Sir William, 14
St Thomas's hospital, 94

The Staffordshire Quarter Session
    Rolls, 130
stains, removal of, 59–60
starch, 55–7
starch, taxes on, 56
stars, influence of, 82–4
Statham, Mrs 130
stockfish, 73
Stonyhurst Salt, 122
Stronor, Thomas
    marriage of child, 7
sugar, 28, 68–9, 78, 147
surgery, 85–6, 88
swaddling, 23, 28
sweat, the, xiv, xv
Swift, Alice, 106
Sydall, Robert, 111

taking your chamber, 21
Talbot, George, Earl of Shrewsbury,
    14
Tedburn St Mary, 8
Tell Trothes New Yeares Gift, 5
Terling, xiii–xiv
Treasury of Commodius Conceites,
    59, 60
Tully, Alice, 130
Turner's Herbal, 140
Tusser, Thomas, 51, 61, 70
Tysehurst, 119

unicorn's horn, 84
upsitting, 24
Urinall of Physicke, 86
urine, 86
urine, as bleach, 55

van den Plas, Dinghen, 55
Van Meteren, Samual
    thoughts on English women, 40
verjus, 74
vermin, control of, 48–9, 51–2
vinegar, 74
Vives, J.L., 37, 140

wardship, 2
washing water, 47, 97
wedding rings, 9
Westminster, 121
wet-nurses, 27
whig, 71
Whitehall, 46, 11
Wilberfoss Nunnery, Yorkshire, 124
Williamson, Joyce, clothworker, 104
Willoughby, Catherine, Duchess of
    Suffolk, xv, 138
Wilson, Thomas, 128
Wimbourne Minster, 127
Winchcombe, John, 110
wine, xiii, 10, 22, 24, 59, 69
wine, care of, 76–7
wise women, 90–1
wool, English, x
wool feels, 104
wool trade, 109–10
woollen clothes, cleaning of, 58
Woulbarowe, Joan, silk woman, 101
Wriothesley, 134

York, 131, 133
Young, Elizabeth, 135

Zouche, Lady, 13